What To Do When Our Emotions Hurt

Lionel Kools

Copyright © 2024 by Lionel Kools

All rights reserved.

Cover Design: Lionel Kools

Interior design: Nikki Mardaga

Interior Illustrations: Nikki Mardaga

Disclaimer:

All rights reserved. No part of this book may be reproduced by any mechanical, photographic, or electronic process, or in a form of a phonographic recording, nor may it be stored in a retrieval system, transmitted, or otherwise be copied for public or private use – other than for "fair use" as brief quotations embodied in articles or reviews – without prior written permission of the author and publisher.

The author of this book does not dispense medical advice or prescribe the use of any technique as a form of treatment for mental, physical or medical problems without the advice of a physician, either directly or indirectly. The intent of the author is only to offer information of a general nature to help you in your quest for emotional, physical, and spiritual well-being. In the event you use any of the information in this book for yourself, which is your constitutional right, the author and the publisher assume no responsibility for your actions.

www.lionelkools.com

ISBN: 9780648847021 - Paperback
ISBN: 9780648847038 - epub

First Edition November 2024

Dedication

A four-leaf clover is one of the most hopeful good luck symbols of the Western World. In shared beliefs, folklore, and traditional superstition, the quatrefoil, under its lucky banner, represents hope, faith, love, and health.

To my son Louis, my daughter Lila, my wife Nikki and I.

Together, we are a lucky four-leaf clover!

Contents

Dedication	III
Acknowledgments	VII
Aperitif	1
Starter	7
Main	21
Everything has an expiry date	23
Create something with a valuable intent	26
Do not repeat your story	30
Where our focus goes, our energy flows.	37
Two ears, one mouth	43
Sizes	46
The snowball	48
Emotional triggers	51
Complexity is made of simple things	54
The power and downfall of labelling	59
Our truth is distorted	60

Wording and meaning	64
Fish and hooks	68
Parenting our inner child	73
Generational downgrade	78
Teen Spirit	84
Get use to life	88
Emotions are life fuel	91
To belong	94
Dessert	99
Compartment One: Breakaway!	105
Compartment Two: Be grateful!	107
Compartment Three: Celebrate our choices!	109
Compartment Four: Create new!	111
Compartment Five: Vibrate our outcome!	113
After Dinner	115
The Bill	119
The Mint	123
Doggy Bag	127

Acknowledgments

First and foremost, I would like to thank you, my readers, for their trust and support. I do not know who you are and the reason that seduces you to select, read, and embrace my book "What to do when our emotions hurt." Everything that you need to know is within you; please use this book as a can opener and discover your magnificent self.

To my wife Nikki, thank you for the trust, support, and your editing and illustrative works.

Aperitif

When our emotions hurt, how doomed are we?

Short answer: We are okay subject to our abilities to adapt and apply new life tricks.

When designing the book cover, I contemplated using a "hangman" illustration for the cover of my book. Why?

Emotions and emotional states have not killed anyone to date. Our emotions management and the lack of it are responsible for our emotional misery, emotional despair and sadly, for some of us, our emotional death.

While drawing the "hangman" cartoon, I hang a lowercase "i" to symbolise the fragility of the mental and emotional "self" and our tendency to exclude ourselves from our sensitive, emotional contents. The "i" is, and must be, our most cherished possession in life whatever our life cycle or our life circumstances. Unfortunately, within the "self", we are endlessly developing and meticulously designing, two personality traits that control intensively and infinitely our daily emotional landscape. Within our emotional shell, we are entertaining with high fluidity two vicious states of mind and operating systems that overrule and destroy the simplicity of "our joyful being". These two statuses are, in no particular order, "self-imposed emotional victim" and "self-imposed emotional perpetrator". Both states are the most atrocious life and existence bashers ever known to the human species.

Anyone, any life experiences or anything outside ourselves can not bash us as much and as harder than the way we self-bash or self-torture ourselves mentally and emotionally. Against our will and the entire content of our emotional intelligence; we are good at being our emotional-self-victim, and we are equally good at being our emotional-self-perpetrator.

We are so good at it that we can condition ourselves to the point of becoming the helpless masters of our emotional destinies. Both states of mind complement another, thrive for each other but overwhelmingly neglect and disrespect each other. As individuals, we are consciously switching from one state to the other. Against the goodwill of our mental health, the content of our emotional intelligence is consistently challenged by self-directed "I am a victim" or "I am a perpetrator" suffocating psychological plays. The frequency and repetition of these mechanical mental patterns corrupt the content of our emotional intelligence and sabotage any attempt of emotional healing. Our inner-victim and our inner-perpetrator persona makes our emotional healing hurt.

Victim and perpetrator are extreme forms of inhuman life experiences; both should not be lived or experienced. What is our aim when we are imposing this type of self-destructive behaviours on ourselves? We unconsciously know that there will be no positive outcome for our wellbeing when falling for our selected "victim" or "perpetrator" persona. Our logic is replaced by a set of mental, physical and neurological habits. These habits kick in as a part of our neurological automated reactive states; our emotional intelligence is always caught on the back foot, and it is not able to acknowledge, react and control our ongoing destructive mental patterns and behaviours on the go. Within all of us, there is not just a single "inner-victim" or a single " inner-perpetrator" identity but a large variety living, evolving, crushing and crumbling our emotional, physical, mental and neurological being.

Having no or little control over our emotional states, we are the puppets of our emotional dependency. We are hooked to our emotional chaos like alcoholics are attached to their alcoholic beverages. We are so entrenched in our emotional mismanagement that we are losing our ability to consider alternative emotional scenarios to trigger our inner built healing empowerment. As dysfunctional puppets, we are repetitively and consistently attaching ourselves to hundreds of rubber bands that are stretching and pulling us in all sorts of emotional directions. These rubber bands are nothing real; they are invisible and an artificial coping mechanism of our emotional world. They are an "on-demand" creative band-aids that are keeping us alive in our self created emotional stories. As we revolve, not evolve, in our ineloquent psychological strategies, we are placing band-aids on our emotional wounds on the go. Band-aid after band-aid we are purposely avoiding any form of healing. We want our emotional wounds to stay raw. Through those we are!

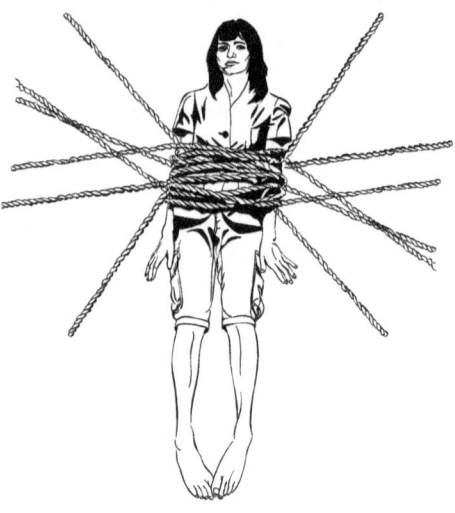

Our emotional habits are the reasons why emotional healing hurts. Our need for control makes emotional healing hurt.

Our biggest life challenge is to maintain our emotional being healthy and to do so we need to learn to navigate with high fluidity between all our emotional states without failing for either a"self-victim" or a "self-perpetrator" status.

Starter

In many restaurants around the world, the menu highlights an array of food categories or meal sections. Chicken, beef, veal, pasta, pizza, soup, vegetarian, gluten-free, starter, main, desserts, drinks, cocktails, pause cafe, beverage, and many more, and we have the freedom to pick whatever selection that will satisfy our thirst and our appetite. We have choices, and it is our responsibility to choose.

When it comes to emotional healing, the process is the same. We have choices, and it is our responsibility to choose. We can read books, listen to podcasts, watch videos, go to seminars and retreats. The options are endless, and like food, emotional healing comes in so many flavours and colours. Emotional healing is a business and an excellent and profitable industry. Millions of humans are seeking mental help, in a form or another, around the clock. So it is our responsibility to choose judiciously what is good for us and what will make us grow mentally, emotionally, and spiritually. A healing journey is a series of choices, commitments, and intents focused on our emotional and psychological desired outcome.

Our choices must consider how to reach our true potential, how to learn to love and embrace ourselves, how to become one within ourselves.

Do not fall for a great marketing campaign, the ultimate aim of an emotional healing journey is to fall in love with ourselves day in and day out whatever the upside-down of our cycle of life. There is no need for Voodoo chants, prayers, tribal councils, and whatever a "buy now" button invites to purchase. Our emotional sanity is always within ourselves, and it is free to seek it.

A shotgun attitude describes best the early days of my emotional healing journey. Unaware of what I was looking for; I was firing right, left, and centre. I was seeking quick answers from numerous sources, and before I knew it, I was more confused. Without this rollercoaster experience, this book will not exist.

Nowadays, through my quest to find something broadly called "happiness", I meet hundreds of people seeking something similar or equal. Looking back, most of us were looking like lost sheep on a mountainside with no shepherd around. Having acknowledged this fact, this makes me realise pretty quickly that my definitions of love and happiness were not universal. Each of us has a different vision and understanding of life, and a unique "happy life" puzzle to complete.

Emotional healing is a personal choice; nobody can force us into it. An emotional healing journey is not a walk in the park or around on the Ferris wheel. It can be hard work, emotionally stressing, and most likely unpredictable as the outcome is unknown. Accepting this fact will help us to make your emotional healing journey colourful, flavourful and successful.

Let's clarify my last word "successful". We cannot change people; we can only change the way we relate to them. We cannot change life "situations"; we can only change the way we relate to them. Success linked to emotional healing has nothing to do with trophies and glory. Our success, which will come from daily practices, is your ongoing ability to be our authentic self whatever the context of your surrounding environment and whoever included in it; and resisting the temptation to fall into the trap of self-inflicted victimisation and perpetrator status.

A quick note on self-inflicted or self-imposed victimisation status as I have experienced it. Before that, I would like to clarify that I am an average "Joe" with no education, no degree in psychology, psychotherapy, psychiatry, and any brain or human behaviours related sciences. As a young adult, I found myself significantly, practically, and mentally ignorant of the reality of life and how to behave outside my early life environments. "Survival" is the keyword that best describes the first twenty years of my existence. Back then, shit was hitting the fan on a high-frequency level. I never knew what to expect. Home was a place with little emotional intelligence on display, and through the years, the shit became even faster and harder. Not long after leaving home, I, unconsciously, self impose a victim status on myself. My story was my identity, and somehow I was secretly in love with this negative projection of the past. My emotional ignorance also became the catalyst for a miserable life.

In my quest for happiness and a better life; I went to a few seminars, courses, and retreats as a part of my early days' emotional healing journey to find a way to deal with my life and its never-ending bitterness. Off the record, I was fucking dumb bad at it. Yes, my words, not yours, but still a few pennies drop. First lightbulb moment: Instant happiness does not exist. Second lightbulb moment: I am not my story, and I was never my story.

These two lightbulb moments made my emotional healing journey suck instantly for a very long time.

Our brain is always excited to receive and process all types of novelties, but its initial excitement wears off very quickly when feeling challenged and under threat. I was facing a nail-biting dilemma to let go of something imperfect and to embrace my unknown emotional potential.

As soon as I commit to the unknown, I realise that emotional healing will suck even more for even longer. There is no way back; emotional healing is a one-way road.

Rest assured (don't burn the book yet), we are, at any time, a world of opportunities bouncing out of some painful life experiences. Our emotional baggage is the foundation of our emotional freedom and the catalyst for emotional growth. There is no life, no liberty, and no grace in a self-victim and a self-perpetrator status. These mental conditionings are only pain on repeat, pain on pain, sadness on sadness, and do not give or allow any room for emotional creativity, blessings, understanding, unconditional love, and self-love!

Emotional healing is the art of falling in love with ourselves and the art of reprogramming years of outdated skills, behaviours, values, thoughts, and habits. Our reconditioning process is personal, quiet, humble, and forever ongoing! Emotional healing has no destination; it is a way of living, an endless quest to understand and appreciate ourselves to our fullest whatever the cycle of life. As a reminder, all the chaos, dramas, and emotional life rollercoasters who enter our life without invitation, are the catalyst of our emotional healing journey. Without these life incidents or accidents, there will be no quest to discover, embrace, and practice self-love. Wearing the self-victim or the self-perpetrator status dressing gown is selfishness at its best. Embracing our past emotional content without a cringe, it is not an overnight success. There are a lot of steps back, sidewalk, tippy toes, and sometimes a few steps in the right direction. Life is an emotional tango in which we should never stop dancing.

An emotional healing journey is personal, what is true or right for some of us will not work with others and vice versa. It is your journey, and it is my journey. The books, the seminars, the retreats are simply a platform, a guide, a helper into our emotional journey. We must do the work ourselves; we can not delegate our emotional journey to anyone else.

I have a say in business: "Business is like a wheelbarrow, if you don't push it, it will never move!" The same principle applies to emotional healing. We need to push ourselves to improve our life, our existence, our present, and our future. Emotional healing does not have a delegation option; all answers are within ourselves, and these answers are only valid for ourselves. We are responsible for our emotional healing, whatever the size of our emotional baggage, and its drama splashed around the place. If we do not accept our responsibilities and commitments into our emotional healing journey, we are most likely to fall back into victimhood status.

Emotional healing, in summary, it is the art of falling in love with ourselves, our true self. There is no better person than us, in the entire universe, who can love ourselves truthfully and authentically the way we understand and appreciate love. We are the only human being on Earth able to love ourselves in a caring manner based on our personal and unique definition of love. Our love definition is individual and mostly based on our past life experiences whatever these experiences were positive or not.

I have committed to my self-healing to seek a better understanding of myself and to appreciate the gift of life. Who I am or what has happened to me, it is not a necessity for my readers to know. I want them to simply imagine me as an average "Joe" who had some issues in his childhood, teenagehood, and, as a consequence, had problems with anger, trust, and a need for recognition. To add to the picture, the average "Joe" as a kid, always knew that something better and attainable exists.

My emotional healing journey started when I was twenty-six years old, and now twenty-eight years down the track, I just started to collect the fruit of my labour. Half of my life, I was trying to acknowledge and understand the mechanics of life and "why emotional shits happen". During this time, I have been challenged emotionally on many fronts, and I lost numerous times the taste of life. Life was tasteless and tasting like poo!

Let me clarify this! Life was not tasteless. I was creating my insipid life; my expectations were creating my misery! I was looking for a quick fix, and the shortcut that I was looking for does not exist. We can not buy happiness; we can not buy love, self-respect and self-love. We need to create it for ourselves! Quick fixes are not working; they are temporary emotional band-aids.

People are jumping to all sorts of addiction to mend their emotional imbalance to feel temporarily better. Healing and greatness are within ourselves; it is our utmost responsibility to seek emotional sanity and consequently love for ourselves.

A variety of emotionally fuelled life hiccups will enter our existence without our consent; these events will "bug" us to a point where indifference can not exist. As humans, we will have an inbuilt ability to seek understanding and answers of ourselves. As humans, we genuinely want a better life, better living conditions, better understanding of our physical, mental, spiritual and neurological being. Seeking answers and clarity is not a one-stop-shop. Pursuing greatness sometimes feels like a can of worms we wish we never opened. Hundreds of questions will see the light, and many of them will have no answer ever. And it is okay; trust me on that one! Not having answers on questions is far less critical than embracing our true self, embracing life, embracing joy, embracing love, embracing and most importantly practising self-love. Valuing ourselves will make our surrounding changes without effort as we do not pour resources and energy into something which has no added value for ourselves. As mentioned above, we cannot change people, we can only change the way we relate to them, and sometimes it also includes putting distance between them and us. We must see ourselves as the number one in our life. Nobody can be above the "I". Applying this principle does not make us a "bitch"; it makes us someone special dedicated to their gift of life.

I was unaware of many things when I started my emotional healing journey. The most obvious of all, I was not aware that there is a parallel universe here on Earth. We are living in a world of duality. For anything wrong, there is something equally correct.

Whatever our life experience, there are two sides to it. Humans have an unlimited power to seek and achieve better life outcomes through the power of mind reprogramming. Mind reprogramming is the universe's greatest gift. As humans, as we grow older, very often we take distance from our universal blueprint and as the gap increases; the universe will play tricks on us to force us to seek and question our existence as a self-loving and self-caring being. As humans, we have little power and control on events entering our lives; we simply have our creative potential to face what comes on offer and use our mental abilities to create the desired outcome through trials and errors. We are here to rise and grow from any unpleasant life experiences. Rise and grow within the power of self-love. There is no need for revenge, vengeance, retribution, retaliation, reprisal, recrimination and payback. In other words; our ego should never be in charge. We can evolve with the power of our heart and within the guidance of our soul and by doing so, we will self-protect and self-bless ourselves emotionally well above our expectations. We should not invest time and energy on outcomes that will not support our oneness and our universal blueprint. Our ego falls into that category; it requires constant management and failing to do so it will exhaust us and turn our life into misery. The gift of life is also to be able to sit on the fence of our life duality and observe from a higher perspective what is right for us. Love and Self-Love are always the winner. We have the freedom of choice, and we will need to make numerous choices to connect to our higher self. Decisions are ongoing. Life is not repeating itself; new challenges will emerge. Every day is a novelty. The more we practice and commit to mind reprogramming as a way of living, the easiest our emotional life will become. Life and its quirkiness are uncontrollable; trying to dominate life is a recipe for disaster. Life is non-boxable; only our mental and emotional fluidity will make us evolve within its never-ending motion and commotions.

When we embark on an emotional healing journey, there is no user manual around or guideline on how to reprogram our brain one on one. My book is a no user manual either. My book is a collection of aha and light bulb moments, tips, tricks and reminders that help my brain reprogram itself as life comes. These aha moments have nothing to do with the harshness of life or the cause of our despair; these light bulb moments are simply magical thoughts accepted as a new standard by our brain. These new reference points are like tsunamis generating unprecedented ripples of our views of the world, life and ourselves. Just like "I am not my story", a few words can be translated into instant freedom and immediate frustration (yes, emotional healing can be painful). Accepting, applying, practising and repeating these new mental patterns, as part of our new behavioural regime, can convert us into emotional freedom on demand! Patience is required; emotional healing is not an overnight success. Our mental circuitry needs adaptation time to accept and validate the new norm.

One of my early mistakes in my emotional healing journey was to gather tons of information and never practice or apply my new learnings. As a consequence, I was repeating the same mistakes again and again and expecting different results. It did not work! The only outcomes out of this useless approach were higher levels of stress, unmet expectations generating high levels of frustration and living a self-created tasteless life.

This book aims to speed up our emotional healing journey with concepts and ideas that can offer alternative psychological perspectives and mental breathing space. As mentioned above, maybe some of my aha moments will not do anything for you, and it is okay. I will not be offended; I will simply cry my head under a pillow. Joke aside; do not discard the new information too quickly, allow space and time for a change. We all learn at a different speed, and sometimes we need repetition to have our penny drop.

The starter is over; time for the main.

Main

Everything has an expiry date

Just go to your pantry and pick up a tin of tomatoes, turn it around and read the expiry date. The can of tuna next to it is the same; it has an expiry date too! Now look around; everything has an expiry date: you, me, the dog, the cat, the flowers. Everything is falling under the same rule; the same principle applies to emotional healing. Our thoughts have an expiry date. Even when we repeat the same thoughts again and again, a day, this thought will die. Something new will enter our brain circuitry and years of beliefs will disappear without acknowledgement or a departure notice.

Any form of actions and reactions also have expiry dates. A lot of us, if not all of us, are or have been subject to single or numerous traumatic experiences during our life cycle. Whatever the severity, the frequency or the harshness of our past and present traumas; a day they will reach their expiry days. It sounds maybe hard to hear or to accept, but everything has a lifetime. "Side effects" of any traumatic experiences such as anxiety, heartbreak, distress, agony fall under the same principle and have an expiry date too.

Nothing on this earth is here forever!

I am aware that some items have a longer lifespan compared to others. Post-traumatic disorders, if we do not address and get the best of them, can be and can feel like a lifetime. Whatever the acuity of misery, grief, heartache, disturbance as human, we have the power, an inbuilt power, to put an expiry date on our hardship. With practice and commitment, reducing the lifespan of our emotional imbalances can be quickly done as turning a switch on and off.

Retraining our brains will also accelerate how things can reach their expiry date well before their initial due date. We have the control; we have the power. It is our choice! Resisting an expiry date is accepting less than our self-worth; it is falling backwards, seeking a status that will serve any purpose except a new cycle of pain.

Let's close our eyes for a moment, breathe deeply and ask ourselves with honesty questions such as: What elements of our lives are reaching their expiry dates? What aspects of our existences have reached their expiry date many moons ago? Are there any characteristics of our daily routines that require their original expiry date to be cut back or shortened?

Emotional healing is all about the comfort of the mind and the comfort to live in peace.

Let's review our plan to gain freedom. After twenty plus years of emotional healing practice, I start to collect the fruit of my labour. Life is not a race; life is an art! Like many of us, I was self-trapped in my thoughts, my actions, my self-sabotage (I could have written this book a long time ago). I thought that paying the rent and putting food on the table was more important than solving a life filled with outdated misery. I have wasted twenty years of service and goodwill just because of a few non-beneficial thoughts. These thoughts only found life and have entertained their power in my weakness. My fake values of comfort blindsided my emotional intelligence. It is well above ignorance; it is slow speed suffocation. It takes more energy to create, entertain and carry a victim's status than it takes to create and enjoy our freedom.

The only expiry date that we should be worried about is the holistic "I".

Create something with a valuable intent

Emotional despair is a natural state of mind, and unfortunately, we sometimes need to experience it to revalue the meaning of our life and our presence on mother Earth. Sadly, emotional despair can also finish as a tragedy. As reported through the news around the world, the number of peoples taking their lives seems like an epidemic. Last calendar year, thirty people took their life in my suburb only. Online data indicates that ten percent of all deaths are suicide-related.

In many cultures, there is no emotional intelligence education. We grow and evolve based, like I did, on our understanding of our narrow vision of life and the world. As a result, it is as good as it gets and we should not be surprised if shits hit the fans left, right and centre.

S.H.I.T.: Small Hiccup In Transit

It takes a village to raise a child and today as we spread ourselves into the suburbs and the big cities, there is less chance to be raised by a community. Emotional intelligence should be a subject taught in kindergarten, primary and secondary schools. Valuing the human experience and the fragility of life from an early age will have tremendous benefit for any individual and all of us as a collective society.

How many people do we know, within our entire existence and life experience, that can say out loud: I love myself, I believe in myself.

As a reader, are you able to say it out loud without cringing or moving like a worm in a compost farm?

I invite you to do it now. Say out loud: I love myself; I believe in myself.

These two sentences are the core of a healthy emotional healing. Our emotional recovery and personal development find its roots in our power to love ourselves and the power to believe in ourselves—nothing more, nothing less. Loving and believing in ourselves is a beautiful and humble experience.

To add to my profile as the average "Joe", I am not a religious person. Loving and believing in myself is sufficient for me. Through the power of self-love, I can access and experience the universe's deepest secrets: Love, life, happiness and trillions of other things. Anything we can not buy at the supermarket are the universe's deepest secrets; they are located somewhere within our neurological circuitry and are accessible on-demand twenty-four-seven like any good, trusted information channels. The word "accessible" does not necessarily mean reachable when wanted or required.

As humans, when the S.H.I.T. hits the fan, and as our emotional despair grows, we start looking within ourselves to seek answers and comfort. Most of the time, we are looking for a quick fix. Something that will make us temporarily better. We just want to apply a smart shinny bandaid on our way of thinking or living that, in all honesty, should require total amputation. The truth is hard to swallow; so we hide our pain into self-created lies that will make us survive to the next crisis. We will invent things to make us great again without knowing that the shadow of our emotional despair is growing bigger and faster than our fake existence made it to the world.

In my twenties, as an average "Joe", I had an addiction to "instant results therapy". This therapy technique, which does not exist, in essence, is similar to a "scratch and win" lottery product. As any form of gambling, our potential to hit the jackpot is very narrow. At the time, I was seeking answers and results without any sort of personal investment and practice. "I want it, and I want it now!" was my motto at the time. I aimed to gain good emotional results without an understanding of myself, without loving myself and without believing in myself. I had crazy expectations! I thought that by reading a book or going to seminars, my life would be "perfect" instantly. I thought that I would receive an aha moment and everything would be alright on the spot. I was living in desperation mode; I was living a deliberate lie. I learned the hard way that a perfect life does not exist. When things started to crash down, I realised that I had a self-centred approach towards myself; I did not include myself in my emotional healing journey.

Emotional healing, like so many things around us, is a formula.

Emotional healing has an origin, multiple contents and inputs, various setbacks, many understanding and emotions, and endless drawbacks and outcomes, no destination and a single purpose: Make us alive again! When we embark on an emotional healing journey, we need to set a clear and valuable intent for it. The ultimate intention is: I love myself; I believe in myself. It took me years of failure to arrive at this conclusion; so I invite anyone to start their emotional healing journey with a simple, livable and enjoyable intent. Most of us are carrying days, months and sometimes years of trauma prior embarking in a recovery healing journey and the potential outcome of our healing journey will be a direct result of our self-loving intent.

When we are emotionally distraught, we are like a racehorse wearing blinkers. Our vision is limited, and we force ourselves into tunnel vision. We have lost our three hundred and sixty-degree view of the world. We have limited our vision to our problems, our pains, our grieves, our bitterness and anything that is not joyful and uplifting. We have removed ourselves out of our life. Within this self-isolation state; we are still responsible for addressing the lifetime of our self-entertained dramas, traumas and despair.

Easy said than done; so I may suggest, as I do not want any of my readers to waste time and repeat unflattering mistakes, to drop our blinding blinkers and force ourselves to put a smile on our face, whether we feel it or not. It can be hard or out of reach, but it is necessary when things hurt. When we share a smile with ourselves or someone; there is a chance of reciprocation. A smile is gradually contagious; this is free healing! I never paid for smiles and their tremendous health benefits. A single smile can change the emotional vibrational frequency of our entire physical body.

Do not repeat your story

We should avoid at any cost to tell and repeat our emotional despair and dramatic story. As painful our story can be, our primary focus in our emotional recovery is to get out of it. Revisiting the stories of our emotional downfalls is addictive. If we are not cautious, this behaviour is most likely to become an addiction just like alcohol, drugs and any form of dependency.

The more we repeat our story, the more its authenticity is altered by the new emotional energy injected into it. So every time we distort our story, we create fiction, and no place or space is available for healing.

By repeating our story over and over, we never leave the starting point of our emotional healing journey. We are passing our entire life in the starting blocks, and we are never running a race.

Quick clarification: emotional healing is not a race; everyone has a different evolving pace. No gold medal or gold star rewards mental freedom.

When S.H.I.T. hits the fan, we try our best to understand what happens to us and talking about it is healthy and essential. We must gain emotional clarity. On the other hand, hanging for months, years or decades on unresolved issues, it is mentally, physically, neurologically, spiritually and emotionally unhealthy! If we are not able to take control of our emotional health on our own, we need to seek help. There are fantastic mental health workers around that have dedicated their lives to make us great again. As a part of their evaluation process, they will ask us to share our story. They need to evaluate the content of our despair but rest assured that at some stage they will invite us, subtly, to value our story and seek an outcome that will serve us well beyond our story.

No repeating our story does not mean no talk or be quiet. Not at all; finding our voice or voices is part of our emotional healing journey. Yes, voices in the plural as we talk to different peoples in different manners with varying intonations of voice. Saying that, we should use our utmost soft and loving voice when we are talking to ourselves. We are not garbage, losers, useless clowns and fucking nothings. It is our utmost responsibility to be generous and respectful towards ourselves.

Emotional crises can find their roots in our childhood and our unloved inner-child, so our emotional beat up must stop with us first.

Instead of repeating our story internally or to any available pair of ears, we should redirect our energy and talk to our inner child instead. With a generous and caring voice, we must help the youngest us to grow out of their fears and mental traumas into an emotionally well-balanced adult. A basic and straightforward way to start an intimate conversation with our inner child is to assure and reassure them that we love them and believe in them for whoever and whatever they are.

We should be generous with our younger self! The more we practice unconditional love towards our unloved inner child, the more chance that our authentic voice will appear.

"I love you; I believe in you" is for our younger self.

"I love myself; I believe in myself" is for the "I" in the present moment.

When we are seeking answers on an emotional level, it feels like we are sitting on two chairs at the same time. Having a half bum cheek on each chair is not a recipe for longterm comfort. One of the chairs symbolises our current environment and its emotional discomfort, and we know that chair too well. The second chair expresses our deepest self-loving wishes and our definition of freedom. The second chair is the one we wish we were sitting on right now. At some stage of our life, we all have our eyes on a second chair, we all know that the second chair will put magical wings on our back and make us fly to freedom again.

Let's be a little bit silly here; practice makes us better. Next time we see two chairs next to each other, let's sit between them and appreciate the fact that we are practically halfway through our emotional endeavour. From that position, let's sit on the second chair and pretend with great enjoyment that some magical wings are attached to our body. Making ourselves comfortable; let's enjoy our new territory, let's enjoy our conquered emotional serenity. There is no hurry! Let's take time to embrace this milestone within ourselves. Let's take time to absorb the beauty and completeness of this self-made freedom. This new feeling now exists only within ourselves and for ourselves. Without any external intervention, our brain is getting reprogrammed; a unique emotional footprint has been created and exists within our mind and neurological system. With practice, we can experience this transformation on demand as much as you wish!

As perfection does not exist; our way of thinking, living, acting and reacting reprogramming content may become the recipient of a variety of useful and useless educational material. Sorting out the mess and the unwanted, and recycling our current and past evolutions is an ongoing affair. Life is not served to us twice the same. So it is better to be ready for changes and constant reprogramming. Not only everything has an expiry date, but everything has only one life. This existence or reality simply exists within the understanding of our inbuilt natural senses and their translated perceptions.

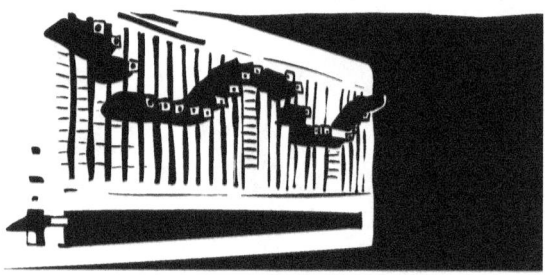

In the eighties and nineties, the stereo systems on the market were available and sold with an inbuilt or separate equaliser. Basic models had a three knob equaliser and the top of the range over dozens and sometimes more. The price tag of an equaliser matches its performance and the number of knobs. Mine had sevens, and a few factory presets such as classical, rock, jazz, ballroom, opera, and so on. Each setup is designed to give us a different musical experience but most importantly, to provide us with our preferred musical interpretation. After acquiring my new equaliser, I have tried all the factory presets and created some custom ones. Within a fortnight, my magical musical genius had selected my preferred way of listening to music. It was not a well-crafted creation of my own; I have simply chosen the "rock" preset on the equaliser. In my "average" Joe's mind, this selection will be the one until I die. Through the years, my musical taste changed and went through all sorts of music genres. To my disappointment, I found the "rock" preset inadequate most of the time.

As humans, will we ever experience reality as our reality? Are we experiencing a poorly translated version of the actual truth? Our universal inbuilt mechanism and senses to experience reality are altered continuously by infinite parameters and presets built and collected through our daily existence. We made valuable choices on the go. Some of them will embrace and mirror our living environment, and anyone included in it and others will rebel to death to whatever is on offer. Whatever our selections, these choices are available for review at any time. Life is not served to us twice the same way. Every day on offer has its variation and an invitation to take control of our life equaliser and to turn the knobs of our life to self-craft an acceptable, liveable and breathable reality.

Charles Darwin (1809–1882) has stated in his biological evolution theory that all species of organisms arise and develop through the natural selection of small, inherited variations that increase the individual's ability to compete, survive, and reproduce.

We are on Earth to experience the gift of life, and this includes the understanding and control of our emotions. The gift of life also embraces the concept of duality within our emotional world. Feelings are not just good and evil; each emotion has numerous subtleties.

Putting Charles Darwin to the test, small variations in our way of living, thinking, acting and reacting within and towards our environment and anyone included in it will give us the upper hand emotionally within and towards that environment. As a reminder, we cannot change people; we can only change the way we relate to them and the same apply to our environment. In an emotional

healing context, our psychological awareness could invite us to decide to stay or to leave our environment and anyone included in it.

An acquaintance of mine said: The grass is not greener somewhere else; it is only the brown dots that are at different places. By experience, I can sincerely tell you that shit does not taste the same everywhere.

Where our focus goes, our energy flows.

To add more to the average "Joe" profile, I fell flat on my face numerous times in my life for small and big things. All types of things, not only material things. Very often, I felt like a "failure on legs with a bleeding nose". The more I was falling flat, the more energy I was pouring and putting into things that will never work. It was all about making the average "Joe" look and feel good at whatever price or whatever cost. At the time, the average "Joe" had a big ego and was craving love, self-love and most importantly, recognition.

Somehow all this was done unconsciously. Did a twisted program hijack my mind? The answer is "NO". I was surviving emotionally, and as mentioned before I was not putting my emotional intelligence at work or at least in practice. Neither says, I was questioning a lot of my progress and downfall but rarely adjusted my course of action towards the right or desired outcome.

A few years ago, and as a part of my roller coaster professional life, I joined a kitchen company as a kitchen sales designer. At the time, I was broke and needed a job urgently to avoid eviction. The first week was all about training and prior the end of day one; I already know that I have joined hell on Earth. My life becomes a playground filled with bullies, big egos and angry bald men.

Through the training, I realise that the top salesmen /saleswomen in the company are clocking seriously good money. As a broke man, the fact that caught my attention was that months after months, years after years, it was always the same guys/girls on top of the national sales leaderboard. Craig, Big Steve and Jack. As a part of the training, I learn about sales performance and company rewards. Top salesmen and top saleswomen had a chance to win a trip to Milan to the Eurocucina international trade show and a safari trip to South Africa. A trip to Italy was my target; no need for a safari when animals are part of the workplace.

Life is a formula and how to climb the national sales leaderboard has its formula. So, I studied Big Steve and had a few conversations with him and picked his brain. Big Steve is a likeable smartass, the king of hard sales, a mind-bender and an outstanding negotiator. I took Big Steve as a role model, and in my head I said: Let's beat Steve and hello Milano!

Easier said than done! Beating Big Steve is hard work! First, I was not a sales guy; secondly, I was not a pushy sales guy. Part of my sales training was to find my sales style and personality while sticking to the sales script. Selling kitchens successfully is a formula! Selling kitchens successfully is an art!

Within eight months, average "Joe" was number four on the national sales leaderboard for the January month without making any "hard sales". Seventeen kitchens sold during the January sales

Main — Where our focus goes, our energy flows.

and a conversion rate under one in three. Being on the road, meeting people, and selling kitchens from dawn to dusk was the best part of the job, on the other hand, my trips to the head office were always filled with some type of emotional uncertainty and anxiety. A way to avoid the unhealthiness of the headquarter was to be transferred to their luxury kitchen division, and I did manage my transfer. Within a year, I have beaten my new colleagues two to one in terms of sales and revenue, and won a trip to Italy.

The best part of the story is not here. Wait a minute and get ready for disappointment and a great life lesson!

At the beginning of the financial year, I created a vision board. Every morning, I was contemplating my vision board; I never skipped a day. My vision board was my screen saver on my computer. All areas of my life had a place on my vision board; I was dreaming big and large. It was the first time that I have included myself in my life's picture. Strange!

The majority of the goals were work and finance related - I was still in a pickle financially, and living on sales commissions only. For the first time ever, I had a goal, and I was focused. For over a year, my focus did not change, and my energy was flowing toward my goals.

Within twelve months, I broke the company sales record. I have achieved my self-imposed sales target, and within a short time after that, I was financially broke again. The company had some production and delivery issues, and the owner has decided to cancel all orders and consequently did not pay any sales commissions.

Yes, S.H.I.T. hits the fan, life hurts, and all types of emotions erupt.

I did learn some valuable life experience from this hard time. I did receive what I have wished for, period! My focus was on my sales targets only; my vision board did not include money landing, staying, and saved in my bank account. Simplistically, I have imposed failure on myself. My focus was not on my financial freedom; my focus was on being the number one salesperson!

So do me a favour: Be very specific, on what you desire out of life, especially when it is related to your emotional healing! A little detail can make a world of difference.

Selling kitchens can be a daily emotional battlefield! In one year, I sat six hundred and sixty-six appointments. Most of the meetings, husbands and wives are present, and most of them are intense emotional games. Within a few minutes, I am aware of who has the power or who to submit to their partner, who is in love, who works as a couple, who has common goals in life, who has emotional issues, who does not give a penny and so on. Humans are "emotional billboards on legs". Through our behaviours, words, attitudes; our inner emotional worlds are on display. As a kitchen designer, I am a couple and relationship therapist! I am inviting both parties to express their requirements, needs and wants. Some clients did not have a voice; they were simply living in the shadow of their partners. Others are playing the power play, such as it is my money; therefore, it is my decision. Others went on strike; no more cooking for you hubby and the list goes on!

The worst experience, I have encountered as a kitchen designer, was an episode of domestic violence. A young couple with two newborn babies were trapped in a messy home renovation with no much money left to afford their dream kitchen. Hell brake loss when the husband has decided to face his wife, and truthfully told her that she can not have the kitchen she always wanted and suggest a two-stage build. Within a split second, everything was flying, verbal abuses were filling the room, and consequently, a two side physical beat up took place in front of their babies.

One of my focus, as a kitchen designer, was not to enter my clients' emotional games and childish behaviours and try, as much as I could, not to take side for one of the parties. My previous emotional failures gave me strong mental foundations to acknowledge the daily load of emotional despairs on display. Still, somehow, it was hard to resist this load of repetitive negative energy and not to fall back into a victim status. Unconsciously I was entering my clients emotional games and childish behaviours as part of my incomplete emotional healing journey. Unsolved past life events triggered their reactive responses. The emotional resolution that I was secretly seeking for my clients was a mirror of the one that I was seeking for myself.

Unresolved emotional contents are like an army of boomerangs spiralling effortlessly into the air, silently waiting to come back and hit us in our core when the least expected. Life dramas will always enter our life without an invite. These uninvited life guest's sole intent is to make us grow emotionally. It is as simple as that! A basic rule of life is to face our unresolved emotional baggage. Ignoring or putting aside our emotional dilemma is asking for more bad things to enter our life. Good things in life are there to be enjoyed, and bad things, especially in emotional and psychological context, are there to be turned into useful learning.

Where our focus goes, our energy will flow; where our focus land is solely our choice, and we can not blame anyone else on this matter. In an emotional healing context, we must focus on something with a higher intent, and we need to take time to analyse, review and revalue our ongoing choices. Any choices that do not support our emotional growth can be changed as much as we want and until we make useful and helpful decisions. We can pick and choose infinitely, and we should avoid choices mirroring or recalling our unresolved emotions and stressful past life events. As humans, we all learn at different speeds, and we all heal at a different pace too. Our healing rate is, often, linked to the readiness of our mind to learn new life tricks. Our mental flexibility and fluidity will dictate the volume, the quality and the integrity of our emotional healing choices.

Two ears, one mouth

As a part of my emotional healing journey, I went to numerous seminars, lectures, retreats, courses and classes. The content of this type of events are an excellent way for learning new life tricks, new methods to reprogram our brain, new techniques to face and address our fears. One of the main aims of all these soul searching events is to teach us how to reconnect with ourselves and how to learn to re-embrace life in a gentle and self-inclusive way.

As stated in the "Starter" section of this book, do not fall for a great marketing campaign, the ultimate aim of an emotional healing journey is to fall in love with ourselves. We joined this type of event based on the hopes portrayed in their marketing campaign. Marketing and advertising have powerful tools and tactics to attract and seduce our senses and leisurely harpoon us within our emotional cores. Our seduction, connection and attraction for what is on offer at this type of meetings need to be explored, experimented, understood and practised. The quest for self-love and self-appreciation is an ongoing life activity.

A great way to explore, experiment, understand, and practice is to connect and interact with other event participants. All participants present at a particular event have something in common. They were attracted to the hope of becoming an "upgraded" version of themselves. It is our responsibility to connect with peoples that will help us in our emotional journey. Not all the participants are beneficial to our evolution. Charles Darwin natural selection theory needs to be applied here. People are energy. It is your responsibility to find the people with healing energy in the pack. I never invite anyone to be selfish except when it is "me" time. It is not every day that we are going out of our way to fix and take care of our emotional content. Surrounding ourselves with positive and energised like-minded individuals is beneficial when upgrading our psychological and neurological operative system. These individuals are forming part of a welcoming, supportive, and self-validated and self-accepted environment. We should avoid at any costs disruptive individuals such as whingers, control freaks, and "Google" on legs as their agenda does not match ours.

My selective approach will probably not work on our first events or emotional healing outings. With practice, we are learning to negotiate our environment and the peoples included in it. Training and interaction with others are open invitations to become a humble, supportive, compassionate and non judgmental healing partner.

Our healing communities can also be silent. Healing does not require words. We can experience the power of healing and emotional healing through numerous love displays such as a caring hand on a shoulder, a warm hug, tears of joy and grateful smiles. Healing and love come in multiple languages.

Learning to shut up and to listen is not an overnight thing. Using our ears versus our month can be an entry point in our healing journey. "To listen" is an alternative way to reprogram and be in sync with our emotional healing's valuable intent.

My book does not intend to offend anyone. Maybe you are the

whingers, the ones who need to repeat your stories twenty-four-seven, the one who wants to take over someone's life, the ones who wants to decide on someone else's behalf. Maybe you are the Britannica encyclopedia on legs or the "google" who have all the answers. Average "Joe" was one of them. He has been humiliated by people rolling their eyes when he was talking, or they were walking away and did not care for what he had to offer. Sadly and in all honesty, at the time, he had not much to offer. His victim status was building a fence around him. There was no open gate for healing to come in and against his will; he was finishing his day with other fence builders.

Our identity reflects our behaviours and the manners of how we conduct ourselves around the clock. Humans like to hold to their personalities; we are creatures of habits. Holding outdated ways of thinking and acting is living in the past that is not serving us and will never serve us at all. As long, our emotional story is alive; we are alive! The reality is that we are dying in the present moment when we are rehearsing our outdated pains.

Sizes

Human behaviour observation is the most fantastic and intriguing hobby in the world. As Average "Joe"; I do not hold any form of qualification in human behaviour. Through my emotional healing journey, I have developed a keen interest in the art of observing peoples. Whatever social interactions, my sensors are deployed and in action. I watch in great detail anyone's body language, facial expressions, and interactions within a defined environment. When having a conversation with someone, I always listen with an emphasis to detect the speaker's emotional drivers, powers, strengths, flaws, shortcomings and weaknesses. Every sentence coming out of our mouth has an emotional underline; some are healthy and some not.

Through my interaction with others and within an emotional healing context; I have noticed a trend which is somehow linked to our expectations and very often described with qualificative and quantitative adjectives.

The trend is: Breakthrough size.

There is no big or small breakthrough in life; there is only breakthrough!

A breakthrough is simply the result of our mind accepting, embracing and validating a new concept or a different way of thinking. These quantum leaps are, in fact, the positive outcome of our reprogramming in action. How we acknowledge or experience a breakthrough can differ for all of us. The feelings, as perceived through our senses, resulting from our inner self-development and self-improvement can feel big or overwhelming, whatever our perception the breakthrough itself has no size. The time it takes for humans to accept a new concept can vary from a split second to a lifetime. In an emotional healing context, our brain will only reprogram itself when we accept and validate our new knowledge, data, environment, and so forth. Our evolved mental comfort resulting from a psychological breakthrough is now a new script and a reference point in our self-managed operating system. There is no way back! The "mechanical" process for our brain to accept our new mental comfort as our new living standard will take less of a millisecond. During this time, the full emotional content of our neurological system is getting upgraded and instantly operational.

As a reminder, we have only one brain, and this fantastic piece of universal technology has the power and privilege to play many roles and functions in our existence. Taking control over our thoughts process, way of living, acting and reacting towards and within our environment and anyone included in it, is our sole responsibility to survive our brain conditioning and procrastination towards changes. Our entire inner operating system, and all its data that define our daily behaviour, is continuously and infinitely refreshing its content. The renewal process of our inner-data is intimately linked to our knowledge, definition, understanding and ongoing life experiences of the word "Comfort". New physical, mental and spiritual levels of comfort are accessible through emotional healing. Living in peace is an active way of living.

One of the biggest obstacles in our emotional healing journey is our expectations. We do not know and will never know what tomorrow will bring us. Life is never served to us twice the same way; there is always a small daily ingredient added into our existence that will make our presence on Earth unique, non-repeatable and priceless. Embracing life with little or high levels of expectations is not living. This form of embracing life is robotic, misleading and full of disappointment in the short, medium and long term. When we expect something in whatever areas of our life, the magic of life will never show up. What makes life magical is the surprise that will surprise us. Removing the fairy touch out of our life is inviting boredom, anxiety and depression into our life. We will never be satisfied with what is on offer to us; as a result, our brain will crave for an experience that does not exist at all except within the unhealthy network of our brain cells. When we drop any form of expectation within our way of thinking, acting and reacting within and towards our environment and anyone included in it; freedom is available instantly.

The snowball

Our perceptions, evaluations and acknowledgement of our emotional despairs is defining the size of our trauma. The reality is trauma does not have size either; there are no big or small traumas. There are traumas!

"My traumas are bigger than yours" is impossible; trauma size competition does not exist! Trauma, as described as a deeply distressing or disturbing experience, has no physical size, shape, colour, not comparable and is individually self-crafted! Adding drama to our trauma is not a healthy healing mechanism to cope with its overwhelming effects on our emotional, mental and neurological being. Qualificative and quantitative adjectives used to inflate the description and the perception of our trama are psychological camouflage. A self-victim status will use this technique, consciously or not, as a call for help or to seek some form of attention and recognition from our living environment and anyone forming part of it.

Whatever the intensity, frequency and harshness of our emotional life experiences; our traumas only exist within the private network of our brain, body cells and neurological system. Physically speaking, our trauma can only be as big as our physical and mental container. Our brain and body cells are the sole recipients of our trauma; outside these envelopes, our trauma does not exist. Someone's trauma is not and can not be more prominent and significant compared to anyone else's trauma. There is no competition in trauma size. Comparing our trauma to someone else's trauma is a waste of time and a sign of voluntary victim status.

Emotional traumas are not contagious; they are only transmissible through our way of living, thinking, acting and reacting within and towards our environment and anyone included in it. A trauma can not be passed from a person to another except if we decide to force it or transmit it mentally and psychologically on someone else.

For some of us, our inner garden looks like a landfill site at the end of garbage collection day. Chaos has taken over. Hundreds, thousands of emotional residues and leftovers are still battling and bleeding all over and within us. Being in that situation; it feels like being in a snowball; an enormous and uncontrollable snowball going downhill, ripping down everything on its way and ready to crash at any time soon. Waiting for the snowball to smash and hoping to survive is self-sabotage. As we are aware of our situation; it is our sole responsibility to take control of our emotional destiny. Chaos is fuelled by chaos; our only option is to get out of the snowball and break our misery life cycle.

In some families, cultures and societies traumas, dramas and illnesses are passed from generation to generation. How grateful our kids should be to embrace the emotional garbage offloaded by their parents, families, villages and society. How can we accept to see the children of the world bleeding, agonising and hurting themselves for something or someone that they did not experience at all? It is our sole responsibility to press the reset button of our emotional life. Getting out of our snowball is therapeutic for the ones who commit to it. As we are committing to our emotional healing, we are offering ourselves and anyone in our proximity a new take on life. Resisting our inner mental freedom does not make sense!

The art of finding happiness is our ability to jump out of snowballs. Awareness is our best asset; as we become aware of our emotional despairs, dramas and traumas, it is our sole responsibility not to repeat them. Emotional healing takes time, practice and patience. It also takes authenticity, humility, humbleness, gratefulness and gracefulness. As much we are living in awareness mode, life events are inevitable and uncontrollable. We have no control over life. Emotional healing aims to gain consistency within our inner emotional behaviours and responses to whatever the outer world challenges.

Emotional triggers

As mentioned in the starter section of this book; who I am and what happened to me, it is not important for you to know. Telling our stories will not help us, sharing insight how to get started and speeding up our emotional healing is far more beneficial. Our stories gave us an opportunity to construct a new level of relationship with strangers who are committing, who have committed, who will commit to a better present and future. Taking control of our emotions in the present is inviting a life with a greater and more peaceful intent.

By telling or sharing our emotional life trauma, we could be the catalyst of emotional triggers for anyone entering and exiting our life. As individuals armed with the powerful gift of awareness, we are not here to put more oil on our emotional fires; we are committed to extinguish our inner demons and discard their ashes. Life is a test and life is ready at any time of the day to test us on our commitment towards our emotional evolution. We will be tested and subject how we are able to stay composed emotionally through these emotional triggers, our better selves will shine. Emotional triggers are the relapse tests during our emotional healing journey. Being emotionally healed is not a black and white process or a straight line. There are no quick fixes in emotional healing. Our self-healing journeys are made of trial and error, acknowledgement, commitment, adjustment, practice, self-evaluation, numerous relapses and lots of emotional triggers along the way to test us in our progress. Emotional triggers must be seen and embraced as friends. Yes, emotional triggers can throw our life around, create mayhem within seconds and destroy our new life foundations without any compassion. As humans, the meaning of our life is to grow emotionally through whatever life experiences are on offer. Our emotional aim is to turn around the unpleasant life offerings into something emotionally balanced. The more we take control of our emotional destiny, the less life turmoils are able to unsettle us.

Have you noticed, I use "We" as much as I can in this book. "We" is inclusive! It is all of us! Do not believe for a moment that the ups and downs of life will spare me of any emotional challenges because I am the author of this book. I do not have any privilege to be spared. I am equal to you. No more, no less!

What we fear in emotional life will come back and haunt us until we face it to its true value. Until we do not address the roots of our emotional discomforts; be reassure that your emotional discomfort will come and bite us again when the least expected. Emotional healing and self healing can be perceived as a multi level video game. We are forced to pass Level one to access Level two. Until we do not master Level one, there is no Level two. Same principle for Level three, level four and so on until we reach Level "Freedom". Each level has its own level of challenges. So it is our sole responsibility to gain new skills to improve our performance, collect rewards and win a game. A common mistake made by emotional healing players, as soon we notice an improvement within ourselves, we stop playing! We have reached a plateau; a new level of comfort has settled in. As soon we become complacent towards ourselves; do not be surprised to retrograde within your emotional healing game. Only practice and ongoing commitment will increase our level of freedom. Praying the universe for a better emotional outcome is seeking uninvited emotional triggers to knock us down to Level one again!

The universe is not a wish delivery service. We are, individually and collectively, the wish delivery service of the universe! The universe wishes are simple. The universe wants us, all of us without a single exclusion, to growth emotionally and to be emotionally healthy. The universe provides us, from the day of our conception, tools and powers to create our emotional wellbeing. He gave us unlimited access to the power of awareness, the power of thinking, the power of relationships, the power of emotions, the power of intimacy and many more. Very often as humans we do not use our universal gifts except when we reach a crisis point. Some of us do not have any knowledge of their inner power and our direct access to the entire universe creation within themselves. The gateway to our universal freedom and utmost emotional wellbeing start with a simple, authentic, humble, truthful, graceful and grateful "I love myself, I believe in Myself".

The more we love ourselves for our trueness, the less chance the universe will tackle down to the ground. Emotional healing is finding the authentic one within ourselves and making it shine without restrain.

I am I for I

You are you for you.

We are We for us

Healing emotionally is easy. We make it complicated. We simply need to acknowledge and embrace our authenticity, humility, humbleness, gratefulness and gracefulness and simply let it shine to the outer world. Be you for you!

When I say: I love myself, I believe in myself. I am I for I in the present moment. The present moment as we experience it, it is a perpetual evolution of time. Every time, I say: I love myself, I believe in myself, The "I am I for I" has already evolved. We can not hold on an outdated version of "I am I for I". Resisting our love evolution does not make sense.

Complexity is made of simple things

When S.H.I.T. hits the fan, we can not predict how we, as humans, will react to sudden and disruptive intrusion into our life. Subject to the severity of the events, our life can be turned into chaos instantly. For some of us, unfortunately, fan throwing S.H.I.T. is a lifetime burden, where intensity and frequency are out of their control. Whatever the type of S.H.I.T. and its frequency, our emotional world could be thrown around and take us for a ride in unwanted or uncharted emotional territories. Whatever the gravity of our emotional turmoil, it is our sole responsibility to get out of it as soon and as quick as possible. Through the power of our emotional intelligence, we have the tools, the resources and the ability to hijack ourselves out of our emotional ordeals.

One of the tools available to us is our ability to break down mentally complexity into simple things. Our emotional connection to our dramas and our traumas can make it worse. So breaking down the emotions and the facts surrounding these emotions is also very important. Nothing is as big as it looks.

When we decide to commit to our emotional healing, we must also be truthful and sincere to ourselves. Whatever our past, we must embrace in its entirety. We cannot pick and choose what we want to address or not. We are living in a world of duality; so there are good and bad in all of us. As humans, we can be the victims of the extremes of life, but by the same token; we can also be the perpetrator of these extremes. Within the right context and the right emotional trigger; the sheep could become a wolf.

Breaking down complexity into simple things. Let's play a game!

Imagine a train network with all stops, stations, signal lights, rails, bridges, switches and sceneries. Yes, the full train set! Let's our imagination run wild and let's make it as big as our wishes. On our train network, imagine a train made of a locomotive and numerous carriages and coaches. The train symbolises the "I" as we are. Our rolling stock includes our emotional journey, and the train network represents life. The carriages and coaches are simply our emotional episodes. As the train travels through the network, some carriages will be removed, added, converted or modified. As mentioned above, the train is a representation of ourselves, including our power of choices. We can decide to go left, right or centre at any time. Our travelling destination is up to us. We are in charge; we are the train driver. The next stop or station is utterly our choices and, as the driver, we should take responsibility for the selection of destination we made. In life and as a generic comment, the only restrictions in our life are the ones we are imposing on ourselves. If we observe our locomotive, there is no or limited reverse gear. Life goes forward at any time.

Now let's observe the carriages. There are different shapes, sizes, some are filled with peoples, others with life experiences, some have an "explosive" sticker on them, and a few are empty flatbeds and so on. Here again, feel free to imagine the perfect locomotive that matches our personality and pick as many carriages as you want. Within an emotional healing context, less is more! The carriages located further away from the locomotive are related to our birth and our early life as children. The wagons closer to the engine, which symbolises our drive, are linked to our present. This carriage order gives us a visual timeline; from early life to today. We are free to shift the carriages and their content as we wish. As our train moves along the track, we, as drivers, are focusing on the present. We are monitoring the rail conditions, the passengers entering and exiting our life, and so on. So, our eyes and focus are not often on the back carriages except when drama occurs, and we are seeking answers and emotional comfort.

The longer the train, the more energy and attention it will require to move forward; consequently, it will also require more significant braking distances when we need to stop. Along the track, there will be signal lights. The reds, the greens and maybe some emergency lights too. Our train and the track network will require some maintenance work from time to time. We do not have any control on the work schedules or the light signals; we must comply with them; this part of our train set is the game or input of the universe. It will force on us some challenges to make us grow emotionally.

Now, let's bring back our focus on the carriages and coaches; they are representing our emotional episodes, including our pre and post conditions to the events. All coaches have front and back bumpers. The carriage's bumpers have some level of flexibility in them and can sustain changes on the go without shearing. The back bumpers, the ones facing towards the end of the train, are representing our emotional predisposition to an emotional episode. The front ones that are directed towards the locomotive, are a representation of our post conditions after an emotional event. As we add or remove carriages or coaches to our rolling stocks during our trips; the front and back bumpers have different emotional and psychological pre and postconditioning subject to the location of the carriages on the train set. We should also consider that if an emotional event is neutral emotionally, there should be no gain or loss between our pre and postconditioning related to this particular event. The carriages and coaches containers represent emotional events within a defined environment, and anyone or anything included and associated with this environment. Our emotional triggers and our emotional states are also forming part of the content of the container. The content of an emotional event will be either accepted, rejected or neutral on the go. Life never stops; so we make decisions, appreciations, rejections, contemplations as our life events roll on.

In our train set, emotional triggers are the ticket controller, and this guy is a freak. Our inner ticket controller can perform a full data analyst of our entire emotional and psychological content. Simultaneously he can compare its findings to the data perceived within the current environment, and instantly rewrite a new set of data that will be our "in the moment" emotional states including all our physical, psychological and neurological changes. The result of this data management, a new set of life guidelines are stored into our front bumpers. This new set of data will be our postconditioning mental state after an event and consequently become our cerebral preconditioning state ready to embrace our next life event. The front bumpers of a carriage is connected to the back bumpers of the next carriage.

When we take a step back and review and analyse the content of our pre and postconditioning, we quickly realise that our inner ticket controller is either a genius or the devil within our mind. All the data coding done on our behalf, by our internal ticket controller, needs to be reviewed, accepted, challenged and reprogrammed if necessary. Our inner ticket controller has a basic and very often outdated operating system, and it is our responsibility to perform an emotional software update. Reprogramming ourselves is a data audit with corrective measures plus a review and changes how we program ourselves.

The flatbed carriages are our mental rest time; we take a step back and voluntarily invite our inner ticket controller to have a vacation and enjoy the scenery. A mental rest time is an active "me" time; we decide to stop our internal mental chaos from being the choreographer of our life. It is our opportunity to observe the way our carriages are organised. With practise, we can discern our living patterns, our life cycles, our type of emotional triggers, and so on. Humans are creatures of habits, and some of them, as we know, are not healthy and beneficial for us. As we take control, the numbers of unhealthy emotional carriages and coaches should decrease as our mental reprogramming will have a domino effect on our old and outdated way of living, thinking, acting and reacting. With practice, our way of acting and reacting will disappear and be replaced by "be" in the present moment. I am "I" for "I" now.

The power and downfall of labelling

Any self-adhesive stickers can easily be removed from any substrate subject to the type of glue used during their manufacturing. Our pre and post emotional conditionings are a collection of labels attached to our life events, facts and beliefs. In our train set example, I mentioned some "explosive" carriages. The word "explosive" is only a word written on a label that has been applied to an emotional event as part of our mental classification system. This type of classification and extreme classification, it is also part of our inner built fight-flight response. Negative labelling is part of our physiological reaction that occurs in response to a perceived harmful event, attack or threat to survival. As part of our subconscious reprogramming, we must remember that every label of our inner classification system has an expiry date. Labelling has a purpose, and this purpose serves us mostly when we are or feel under threat. As we commit to our emotional healing, we must face the fact to rip stickers and labels off our belief system.

When we question the value of our emotions and our emotional labelling system, we should treat them as something for sale on a supermarket shelf and apply a market value to the entire content.

Our whole emotional catalogue is now facing the reality of the marketplace, and our pricing is subject to supply and demand, customer expectations, market conditions, and so on. Quickly, we will realise that there is no demand for our self-designed emotional catalogue. As our items stay on the shelves, and no one buys them, their conditions and values are diminishing as time goes by. As we hold onto our belief, we decide to create marketing and sales campaigns and here again, our emotional items are still not moving. The prices on the labels are falling down and prior we know it, there is no profit in this venture; we are at a loss. Holding any further will makes things worse.

The value of our outdated emotional content has only value for ourselves. The more we hold onto it, the less value it has. The more we hold onto our beliefs; the more we devalue ourselves and our life.

Our truth is distorted

When breaking down our emotional episode, first we should acknowledge our pre-condition to an emotional event. We all do not relate to context and situations the same way; our personal psychological, physiological, neurological and spiritual state, and emotional baggage influence how we enter and manage our emotions.

Life events are two parts. The first part is the reality, which is displayed to us through a series of sensory experiences (visual, sound, smell, touch, etc.). The second part is how these sensory experiences are instantly processed and perceived through our emotional know how personal database. Every life event will be seen, appreciated or rejected simply based on our understanding of past life experiences. We have inbuilt parameters within our way of thinking, living, acting and reacting that will decide if an event will be, instantly, catalogued as traumatic, enjoyable, challenging, and so on.

Our emotional catalogue is stored within the cells of our physical body; the way we catalogue our emotions is unique for every individual. The content of our psychological directory is a reflection of our entire life experiences and events; from our early life upbringing to this present moment. In "our train set" example, the ticket controller is the one in control of the majority of our preparation towards future emotional events and their outcome.

Knowing that our inner ticket controller is a very busy guy who does not have great eyes for details, and like all of us, he has got its mind and personal agenda. Can we trust him?

Is our emotional content an array of inaccurately transmitted distorted truth? Or does our psychological content consist of numerous sequences of repetitions of a story, each one differing slightly from the original?

Let's play an inner Chinese whispers game.

Imagine a table with ten chairs, and on each chair, there is a copy of ourselves seated around the table ready to play Chinese whispers. What will the final result be? Probably not as authentic as it should be. This is what happens when we let our inner perception take over our emotions and emotional content. Our internal content becomes a distorted version of our inner truth.

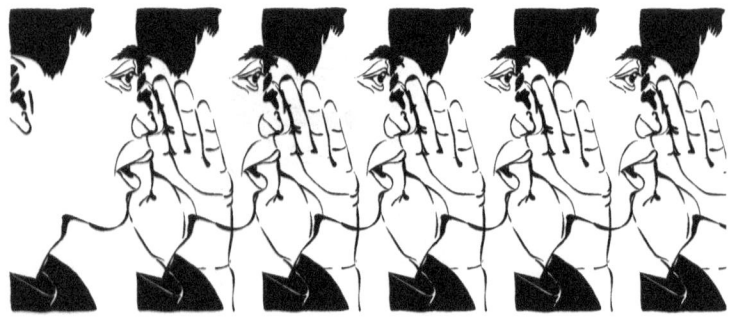

As an average "Joe", I have repeated numerous times my emotional story. Subject to the environment I was in, and anyone included in this environment, I have noticed subtle changes in the content of my story every time I was outpouring my emotional relics. It does not sound like a big deal except when we consider that we have created distorted or false emotional events that will be classified by our inner ticket controller as our new emotional and psychological benchmarks. The parameters of our new guidelines have their roots in our inner misery, the instant feedback of the environment we were in, and the imperfection of our emotional classification system.

As a result, the thoughts within our minds do not necessarily equate to truth; even if they exist and have residency within our belief system for some time. Repeating or activating the same thought, again and again, will not make true or real. The opposite will happen. We use our thought process as a vehicle to go around life without really supporting our emotional being. Our thought processing is somehow a reflection of our selfish self "instant gratification" survival mechanism. We want to feel good instantly without addressing the underline of our emotional disorders.

There is no hardness, harshness, inflexibility, rigidity, rigidness, rigour, rigorousness, severity, sternness, strictness in truth. Truth has a fluidity; Truth is fluid. Our identity and more specifically, our emotional identity and status should embrace and reflect the fluidity of truth and reality. There is no container able to contain truth. The creative power of emotional healing journey is available through our connection to truthness. The more we practice "I am I for I", the more truthness will shine within ourselves and consequently will affect our outer world. We can not change people; we can only change the way we relate to them. This fact is a two-way street. Our external environment will be forced to heal to keep us within their inner circle.

Wording and meaning

As we speak, we assume that the content of our conversation will be understood with clarity by others. This type of assumption is not helpful; each of us has limitations. Our habits are narrowing our hearing decoding abilities, reduce access to the vocabulary at our disposal, and have applied a particular and distinct meaning to our vocabulary. We will never use the entire content of a dictionary as a part of our interaction with others or within ourselves. Much of the wording used in our daily activities reflect the filters and processes of our catalogued past emotional states; this means that only a small number of words are used and repeated. The essence and content of our conversations are intellectually instantly distilled into something that only makes sense to us emotionally, and this bundle of new emotional data is automatically forming part of our current psychological acceptance and emotional benchmark.

The meaning of the word "love" is individual and specific to any of us. No one can love us the way we want to be loved and; no one is better than us to define "love" the way we like to experience it. Within an emotional healing context, it is our responsibility to broaden our understanding and vocabulary spectrum to let words such as "love" evolve to another level of understanding. By doing so, we can experience "love" to new levels of intimacy.

As an example, the word "intimacy" is linked or referenced, for a majority of people, to sexual intercourse. Within an emotional healing context, intimacy and self-intimacy is about closeness, togetherness, affinity, rapport, attachment, familiarity, confidentiality, friendliness, comradeship, companionship, affection, warmth and understanding. Self-intimacy is the art of being aware of your feelings and emotions. Each emotion and feelings have their meanings within our inner, personal and intimate archiving system. Each of us has the power to experience, understand, express and radiate through our emotional interactions. Today's emotions are a reflection of our processed past; our emotions perceptions, definitions and meanings that require ongoing revaluation through our combined power of awareness and our self-commitment to changes. The more, we love ourselves and the more we commit to ourselves, the less chances we have to experience inner chaos. Loving ourselves is building up our emotional immune system, and it is also training our emotional intelligence to avoid out of proportion emotional reactions when hectic and detrimental events enter our life. Questioning and embracing the entirety of our feelings and emotional states, whatever the label, stigma and hurts attached to them, is the core of self-growth, self-love and self-healing. As a reminder, there are no right or wrong emotions. There are only badly labelled emotions, and our attachment to them can make them toxic. Our intimate relationships towards and within our emotional content will define the outcome of our emotional states. We need to educate ourselves on why our inner classification system has fallen in us in the first place and how we can avoid future emotional snowballs.

As an average "Joe", I have migrated from Europe to Australia in the mid-nineties. Within six months in the Skippy world, the honeymoon period was over and the magic of my new country had already lost its shine. My focus was on the downfall of the green and gold country. Where our attention goes, our energy follows. I became critical, bitter and somehow arrogant. Nothing on offer was able to match my superior standard. Everything was classified "shit" and "fucked". The reality is that everything can not be just "shit" and "fucked". My two words basic classification system evolved when I decided to look inside myself during a mental breakdown. The three words that best describe the outcome of my psychological introspection were: Sadness, loneliness and disappointment. At the time, I was sad, lonely and disappointed. My "shit" and "fucked" antics were a necessary call for help.

We can be shocked when we realise how basic our cataloguing system is and how it works. We are creatures of habit, and we also have a lazy tendency when addressing our mental processing faculties. We often embrace the lowest common denominator when it comes to our mental wellbeing.

When we start observing our surrounding environment and anyone included into it, we become aware of our individual and collective ways of thinking, living, acting and reacting and most importantly the footprint of society on us. Every day we are getting bombarded by political, cultural, spiritual and commercial issues that impact our emotional being. Music is also an excellent platform to heal or to sink emotionally. The words and meaning of the song going through our ears can have a profound impact on how we condition ourselves mentally, physically and spiritually. Lyrics and meaning can make or destroy ourselves equally with the same force; just a few notes played on a keyboard can create social uprise, cultural revolution or gently put a baby asleep. Music genres such as hip hop and rap convert their loyal fans emotionally through the power of distorted words, baffling meaning, unethical grammar style and a subtle game of out of context references. Rap artist's offerings are well crafted emotional statements. We all have a heart. The complexity of some artist craftsmanship requires translation for the non-expert listener in this type of music genre. Words, meanings and conversations in foreign languages and their subcultures can lead to inaccuracy in our interpretation of their content subject to our knowledge of the language and the cultural, social and ethical context of the conversation. This inaccuracy in translation will become the baseline of our future understanding.

As a listener, it is our sole responsibility to seek clarification when we do not understand the content of a conversation. Even a single word can be the centre of awkwardness. Confusion has no benefits and can quickly become a catalyst for unwanted emotional triggers. As a listener, it is also our sole responsibility to seek clarification on the tone used in a conversation. Words can have an emotional impact, but the tone used to say them can be more devastating.

Fish and hooks

What on earth, fish and hooks have to do with emotional healing?

Let's imagine a vast ocean full of fish and on the surface of the water, a few boats with their fishing rods ready for actions, hooks and baits dancing through the currents of the pristine water. In this analogy, our emotions states are the fishes and the hooks our emotional triggers. Our emotional states are always free and neutral until something catches their attention and lures them away from their freedom. Freedom was there all the time, but somehow, we decide to get hooked and relinquish our emotional freedom on unworthy sensitive matters. If we review the scenario of how we are losing our emotional freedom, we should address our inadequate emotional intelligence energy management and our intimate and self-developed relationships towards our emotional hooks. On this matter, there are three basic scenarios: we are attracted to the hook, the hook draws us, or there is a reciprocal attraction between us and the hook.

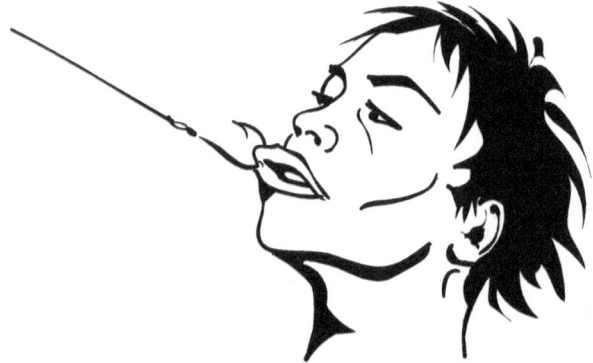

Whatever our preferred scenario and its outcome; our emotional life will be changed forever. Our life experiences are designed to make us grow emotionally; which is the primary purpose of our presence on earth

Fishing has rules, regulations and quotas. One of the rules is related to the size of the fish. Small fish will be thrown back into the big pool of freedom filled with potential hook hazard, and unfortunately, bigger fish are finishing on our dining tables as sushi and sashimi. In the fish world, it seems that things get tougher as the fish becomes older or bigger. In our reality, size and age do not matter. We should embrace our emotional intelligence as soon as possible and improve it as we practice life. Unresolved emotional matters are subject to compound effects. Shit becomes shit on shit. If not tackled shit on shit will turn into shit on shit on shit and so on. Do we want to swim in a pool filled with poop?

Knowing that only small fish in size are thrown back into the big pool of freedom, how can we gamble our freedom knowing that our freedom is within the fisherman's hands and his understanding of the fishing laws and his willingness to enforce it. The fisherman mental fish processing method is simple as "Yes-No" or "Good-Bad" or "Big-Small". There is no mucking around on a fishing deck. Acknowledging this fact, are we still interested in playing the fishing roulette? Reviewing our life patterns and cycles, how many times do we fall back for the same hook, the same problem, the same outcome? How many times do we lure ourselves into false, fake and inexistent realities? How many times are we bluntly lying to ourselves? "Less is more" should be our aim. Every time we blindfold ourselves emotionally, we are hurting ourselves. We design and craft our pain; to make it even more painful we believe in it, we experience it, and we become the projection of our crafted pain. As we repeat this process again and again, we are our pain. Our pain is now our physical, mental, spiritual identity and is catalogued as our emotional benchmark and its footprint can be found within our entire cellular body. We are the only one to blame for our creative egoistic emotional pain. Our pain design is so clever and so believable that it turns and comforts us into a victim status. The pain inflicted by our environment and anyone included in it is far less painful than any pain generated by our emotional misunderstandings and the poor management of our emotional intelligence.

Let's go back to our love attraction to our emotional hooks. We are attracted, they attract us, and there is a mutual attraction. Whatever our choices, we are in trouble. What makes us jump the wrong emotional wagon knowing that our freedom and faith will be decided only by the fisherman and his fishing rules or fishing quotas. The trick to avoiding a self-created emotional crisis is to press the "pause" button and ask ourselves two simple questions: Is this for me? What do I want out of this experience? We are so used to living at a fast pace and reward ourselves instantly that we forget our power of choices and our magic ability to delay drama entering our life. The "pause button" is awareness in action. Peace and serenity are our ultimate goals, not chaos.

If Charles Darwin was invited to give some guidance to the school of fish to secure their ongoing freedom and evolution, what will be his suggestions? Let's go wild here!

Idea 1: The fish mouth should be relocated on the side of their face, so the hooks can not get them.

Idea 2: All fish must have some tiny hands and fingers around their mouth area; this added feature will permit the fish to unhook themselves well before catching the fisherman's attention.

Idea 3: Fish should be blind or eyeless.

Whatever ideas, Charles Darwin would not suggest or change a single physical attribute of the fish or any other species. Based on his observation, he acknowledges that our relationship to our environment and anyone included in it is the primary catalyst for changes and if any modification is required, physical or not, it will be solely made by the power of our mind.

Creating a victim status or designing our emotional evolution requires the same amount of mental energy. The initial implementation of either scenario will also require similar mental energy. The ongoing practice of either scenario will differ dramatically as evolving towards our true self is less painful and less tiring physically and mentally. A self-victim or self-perpetrator status is a self-imposed burden on ourselves. We are adding weight on our shoulders for nothing. As we commit to our martyr status, we are less mobile. We are getting stiffer; we are losing our mental and physical flexibility.

At any time, our physical body is the mirror of our thoughts and emotions, and his youth is preserved by the way we love ourselves. Our emotional intelligence energy is radiating in every cell of our body in a positively or negatively charged frequency. "I am I for I" is the best healing energy policy for our physical body. When we love ourselves, we lower our body frequency, and automatically we are preserving ourselves against the corrosive effect of our living, thinking, acting, and reacting mechanism.

When we are taking time for introspection to seek an understanding of our life cycle, thinking pattern and so forth; we will acknowledge very quickly that most of our life we chew the same bait and similar types of hooks. When it comes to our understanding of emotional and overall well being, we are not always creative.

As an exercise, let's imagine that we are invited to visit a fishing gear supplier to catalogue our emotional content. One hundred hooks are on display; twenty horizontally by five vertically. The hooks come in twenty different colours and five sizes. Each colour will represent an emotion and the hook size its intensity or frequency.

As a point of reassurance, there are no right or wrong answers. The results will represent a snapshot of our individual life experiences, our emotional story, emotional focus and emotional traps. What is interesting to observe during this exercise is our initial physical and emotional reactions as we categorise the hooks and how quick some of the labels [I hate this word] come along. The most extraordinary fact of this exercise is that we are unable to label twenty emotions types of the cuff. This incapacity is linked to the narrow view of our emotional world. We are focusing on a small part of our picture but not the full picture.

As creatures of habit, we sustain our emotional relationships to our pain as our primary survival tools. We believe that we only exist through the potency of our story; we believe that our story is our identity. As a part of our mind reprogramming commitments, it is essential to understand our living, thinking, acting and reacting patterns and why we are addicted to particular emotional hooks. If we have a psychological addiction; we should acknowledge it and seek a resolution for it.

Labelling the hooks is similar to weighing ourselves at the beginning of a diet or a weight loss program. This is our starting point, and from there, we can design the life we want and embrace our true self and our unlimited freedom.

Looking back on life, the average "Joe" has wasted a big part of his life on a few hooks and the stories attached to them. All this time, his story was an addiction, and everything was painted with the same brush. He took him a very long time to ask himself two simple questions: Is this for me? What do I want out of this experience?

Parenting our inner child

One of the reasons we are repeating the same life cycle and same thinking patterns is the lack of parenting towards our inner child. As young children, we were, for the majority of us, surrounded by adults who had the "responsibility" to raise us and to love us. Some of them did an outstanding job, some of them did a good job, some of them did an okay job, some of them did an average job, some of them did a poor job, and some of them did an awful job. Pointing the finger towards these adults and blaming them for our emotional downfalls and emotional states will not resolve anything. So it is better to look inside and find out how we want to be loved and how we need to correct our inner child parenting patterns. It is our sole responsibility to adjust and tweak our inner self and feelings. Wasting time, money, energy and resources into a blame game will not solve anything. There is no user manual of how to raise a kid or how to be a kid. There is also no user manual to how to be the perfect father or the ideal mother. Life comes unprepared; we need to create and adjust to the content of life and make it perfect through its imperfection. We have no alternative than to discover our true self by ourselves through our inner creativity.

Adults who had the "responsibility" to raise us and to love us also have unfinished emotional healing business. How are we able to love someone else when we do not embrace ourselves fully. Self-love is an ongoing practice and has no completion date. Self-love is never-ending; it is our responsibility to keep it up to date through the challenge of our life. When we love ourselves; we are projecting respect towards us.

Whatever our upbringing and its emotional harshness, we cannot look back and blame others and ourselves for what happened. Life only goes in a forward motion. Going forward is an invitation to let our creativity reinvent ourselves days after days. Our self-regeneration abilities work only as an "on-demand" service; when and where is needed and most importantly, when and where we want to give it a shot. At any point in our existence, we have the power to press the "reset" button of our life. We have unlimited chances to recreate ourselves emotionally and to become "I am I for I".

Our long term emotional imbalance could find their roots in the data stored within our inbuild emotional and psychological cataloguing system. Life creates events, and we process these events into memories, and we relate to these memories, including their emotional fuel, as our truth. For these memories to be our "present" truth, we must access them with honesty and question the core of their emotional contents. Memories are part of our story, and the more we access them, the more they will be distorted to fit our "feel good" daily emotional agenda. Every time our inner child is crying for love and attention; we must take time to console, comfort and love it unconditionally. As hard as it sounds, we need, as part of our love and attention towards our inner child, to parent it and most likely to discipline it. Our inner child is running wild and is playing all tricks in the book to seek our and anyone else attention. The most significant gesture of love towards ourselves is to discipline our mental representation of the younger us. Our inner child only exists within our perception of our distorted memories and the environment included in these memories and anyone forming part of this particular environment.

When we observe, with honesty, our ways of living, thinking, acting and reacting within our environment and anyone included into that environment, we quickly realise that the majority of emotional behaviours are little toddler's style; which is basically "my way or the highway". In the early years of our existence, our emotional intelligence is not fully developed to comprehend the life on offer. Whatever our comprehension or not, our inbuilt emotional cataloguing system has translated the content on offer into a script that makes no sense to anyone, including ourselves. To our astonishment, this script is running as the baseline of our emotional operating system.

As much we consider ourselves as adults, we simply are the puppet of our six, seven or eight years old self. Our inner child is playing the strings of our daily emotional behaviours. Only the power of awareness and our willingness to change can pause or stop this type of automated emotional response. As soon, our consciousness is catching ourselves into our repetitive and emotional mischiefs; we need to pause our life and take time to address these matters with our younger selves. We are not here to punish our inner child; we do not want pain on pain. We are simply here to give comfort, love and give our younger selves an update on today's reality and invite him to converse freely and express his feelings and discomforts. By providing self-love and attention to our inner child, we are providing the parenting style that we, as children of all ages, including "adult kids", are craving for unconsciously. Only "I" know the way, we want to be loved, cherished and appreciated. Inviting our inner child to express his core emotions safely is only a third of the process. The second third is to express our today's feelings and emotions openly to our inner child and let the conversation flow to discover our point of difference and how we can find a common and beneficial way of living, thinking, acting and reacting. The third part of the process is to reduce the gap between our fundamental point of views, past and present, on how we want to be loved and how we can amend our survival patterns and feel safe afterwards. By doing so, we discipline our inner child through the power of love, and as we do, we establish guidelines, understanding, mutual respect and trust within and towards ourselves. Letting go of our inner identity is one of our lifetime biggest fears.

Connecting with our inner child requires patience and practice. The three-part process must become an ongoing and "on the go" life practice. There are no quick fixes. Establishing a loving connection with our inner child is not a guaranteed success. It is all about trials, errors and sometimes rejection.

How will we react to someone who has ignored us for ten, twenty, thirty, forty, fifty, sixty, seventy years and more and, suddenly and out of the blue, declare his/her love to us? Our inner child and ourselves can be strangers, even living and being the same identity.

When connecting to our inner self, our first hurdle is not to compete with our childish primary script that runs the baseline of our emotional life. This primitive behavioural script is also the container of our victim status and our ego. When our ego takes control of any life events, love melts away like ice cream in the sun and S.H.I.T. will hit the fan well before we know it.

As an average "Joe", I have two kids. My son is turning twenty-two, and my daughter is a sixteen. As a father, I love them dearly, and part of my love expression towards the two of them; I like to remind them the following: I love you, I love you to the best of my ability, I love you the way I understand love, and I love you knowing that my love towards you is maybe not the way you want to be loved and appreciated and whatever your stand on my love, I love you.

As an average "Joe", I am no love guru. I am not much at all; I am just an ordinary guy who decided to address his recurring emotional episodes. Emotions are part of our life, and we must experience them to their fullness whatever their origin, spectrum, depth and intensity. By addressing my emotional downfalls, I have created an approach to establish an equilibrium into my way of living, thinking, acting and mainly reacting. As a part of this approach, I will do my utmost to avoid and to repeat the extreme of my emotional life whatever life throws at me, whatever the environment I am in and whatever who is included or forming part of this environment. When my awareness notices, usually through a mental and physical unease, a non-beneficial "deja vu" emotional response, I pause for a moment and ask myself three questions this time around: Is this for me? What do I want out of this experience? What do you think?

The "what do you think" question is intended to my inner child, inner self and my higher self. I never expect an immediate response. I like to be surprised by their input and feedback, and very often, they surprise me when the least expected. The answers I received are a combination of all versions of myself. The answers are matured answers. They don't promote inner conflict, inner chaos, pity or any negative feelings towards myself. I am not interested in playing the detective to find out who has provided the answer; I am only interested in my emotional growth and my mental wellbeing. Validating my inner child, my inner self and my higher self through their feedback also reduces the gap between all versions of my inner "me" and helps me to become and ultimately be "I am I for I".

Generational downgrade

I do not believe that we are coming to life emotionally pure. We are not born emotionally empty or without any emotional footprint or any types of psychological activities. From the moment that we are conceived; we are emotionally loaded. Babies' emotional contents are the mirror or a diluted version of their parent's emotional identity that reflects and summarises their individual and collective journey and life experiences.

The quality of the pregnancy is altering and affecting our initial emotional load. The mental and emotional states of our parents will contribute massively towards our early psychological development. The child bearer, which has the most influential relationship with the baby, is probably the main contributor to its early psychological evolution. The environment where the pregnancy is taking place and anyone included in it also has a significant impact on our mental aptitude.

The world population is over seven billion people, and none of us is born emotionally perfect, gifted or balanced. Average"Joe" is no exception!

We are born emotionally challenged. In addition to this reality, life, with its unpredictable agenda, will add its emotional burden to the mix. All humans, without exception, will need to address somehow, at some stage of their life, their emotional downfalls to enhance their quality of life and the quality of their inner relationship with themselves. Practising emotional healing as a daily activity will contribute towards our inner mental comfort, self-acceptance and self-love.

As children, our primary emotional learning mechanism is by soaking up whatever life has to offer. The first few years of our life, we are acting like little sponges; we are absorbing. Whatever the content of our early life within a family environment, or not, will be the foundation of our understanding and footprint of our future emotional being. As we grow up and increase our interaction with siblings, other kids and adults, we are gaining a broader view of our environment and anyone part of it. By the age of six, seven or eight; our early emotional footprint has already been processed as the baseline of our present and future emotional life. This little script in our operating system is ready to challenge us joyfully our entire existence. This small piece of inner coding is our reference point of how we understand life and the world around us. Somehow we like, consciously or not, to hold to this marvel of our imagination. As we keep growing up, through teenage years to adulthood, we are forced to reprogram ourselves on the go and to review, adjust and tweak our emotional anchors, beliefs and understanding. Our psychological evolution requires some serious choices to be made. One of these choices is essential and can be summarised as: "adjust or be in pain" or more dramatically "adjust or die".

Pain and pleasure are extreme in our emotional language and life experiences. Both do not have the same intimate relationship within ourselves. One is a free agent, and the other is more likely to become a lifetime addiction. As humans, we never complain about pleasure, happiness or too much joy in our life. Pain has the opposite effect and makes the majority of us whinging about our self-created sufferings.

The origins of our emotional disorders, pains, understandings and misunderstandings can find their roots within the habits of the previous generations forming our family. Like our DNA, they were transmitted to us without our consent.

As an average "Joe", I had the privilege to experience and observe four generations living under the same roof. For financial reasons, my family and I were forced to move in with my mother-in-law. At the time, she was the primary carer for her mother. Except for individual life experiences, there was not much difference how three generations of ladies were operating emotionally, individually, collectively, and how these three ladies relate emotionally towards my son.

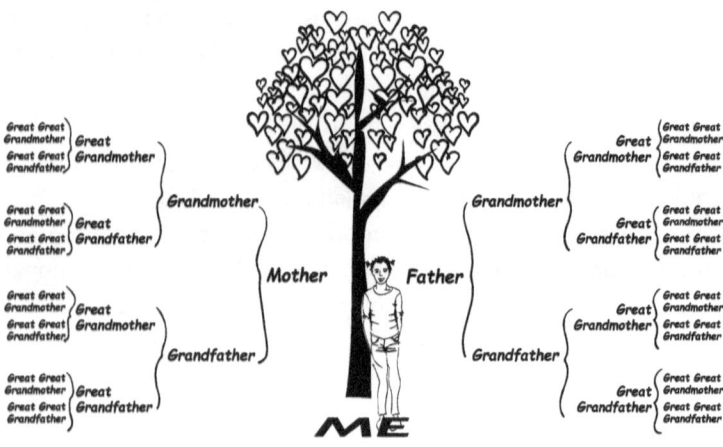

Based on this observation, let's our mind run wild for a while. Let's imagine a family and each generation forming part of this family had their kids at the age of twenty-five. "Twenty-five" is selected for mathematical easiness. As the fifth generation is coming to life, one hundred years separate the newborn to their great-great-grandfathers and their great-great-grandmothers. Within an emotional context, is there a point of difference between the great-great-grandparents and the baby? To push it a little bit further; what is the difference between our ancestors and ourselves. Well, not much at all is the answer. If we push our observation to a cycle of two hundred years, three hundred years, and so on; we quickly realise that our emotional intelligence is primitive indeed. Hundred years seems a long time, but it only takes thirty-one individuals to form a five-generation cycle. Our DNA and our intergenerational emotional footprint are our strongest, most durable bond and connection towards our genealogical ancestors. Acknowledging this fact should put some perspective into our emotional journey and its content.

Each generation made it through their environment and life experiences and as a result; a big part of their emotional baselines are reflecting in their unique interactions with their environment and anyone included in it or forming part of it. Based on our twenty-five years generational cycle over a period of hundred years, it took thirty-one people to deliver a single unique individual. The way to embrace and maintain our individuality through our entire existence is simply by cherishing what is valuable to us, and throw away the unnecessary garbage out and replace it with something more palatable to our inner feelings.

As a snapshot, our emotional content can be perceived as a jar filled with a mixed selection of lollies, and whatever happens in our life, the jar is always full. Our emotional healing aims to secure the perfect lollies selection within our jar. To do so, we are forced to take out the lollies that we do not want and replace them with the lollies we want. Lollies trading is the only process that will achieve the perfect lollies mix based on our individual selection criteria. As life is always served to us in a forward motion, the snapshot becomes a movie. Life has its own speed and will not wait for anyone. So we are forced to add and remove lollies from and to our jar on the go, and most importantly, we are not allowed to tip our jar upside down to sort out our likes and dislikes. Some of our unwanted lollies will take more time to get out of the jar compared to others subject to their location and access within the jar. As time goes by and to reflect life's ever-changing evolution, our lollies taste will also evolve and consequently force us to amend the content of our jar accordingly to our forever changing taste bud. Some lollies, going in or out of the jar, are stacked together; they represent the domino effects within our emotional healing process. Numerous emotional issues are solved at the same time. Stacked lollies must be seen as magical moments in our emotional healing journey; as we are not able to take them apart and they must be processed as a bundle either on their way in or out of the jar.

When we take care of ourselves and love ourselves, life magic will shine, and unexpected domino effects will arise on the go whatever the environment we are in, and anyone included or forming part of this environment.

Trading our emotional content is very often a trial and error process as we decide to replace outdated items by new things that will not necessarily fit our emotional purpose either. A simple example is the number of ex-girlfriend or ex-boyfriend that have crippled our love life as a part of our quest for love. Some relationships exit our life in a blink of an eye, but some cannot. Whoever enters our life comes with the sole purpose to make us grow emotionally. Accepting this fact will save us time, money, resources and pain. So, let's repeat; whoever enters our life comes with the sole purpose to make us grow emotionally.

All human relationships forming part of our lives are not necessarily our choice. Our family was imposed on us, our friends are most likely to be our choice, and our social network and social environment look like a ping pong game; they are coming and going with or without invitation. Whoever enters our life, we can decide the way we relate to them; nothing in life is imposed on us forever. We have the freedom to choose what is right for us and sort out the drama out of our life.

We are over seven and a half billion humans currently living on earth, and all of us come from a particular type of dysfunctional family. They are no exception even if our family looks spotless, shiny and sparkly clean. As much we believe that we are unique, we are not. From the moment of our conception, we are already carrying our ancestral emotional baggage. History, and most likely distorted history, is already within us. Our uniqueness comes from our life experiences within our living environment, and anyone included and forming part of it and most importantly, the way how we process, accept, reject the life on offer and its environment. Emotional trading requires patience, skill and commitment to unseat and heal our emotional trauma whatever they are imposed on us or self-created. Some of us have experienced the extreme of life such domestic violence, verbal abuse, physical abuse, sexual abuse, rape, war, holocaust, genocide, slavery, confinement, mind games, financial distress, bullying, heartbreak and much more. Our aim in life is not to survive life. Our objective is to embrace our freedom and discover our true-self through the burden of life.

As a side note, we must distance ourselves, mentally and physically, as soon as possible from any type of hostile environment and anyone included in it. There is no beauty in emotional and mental chaos.

Whatever the harshness of life we endure or have endured, we must find, accept and embrace the positiveness of these events. We are not our story; we are only the victory of our commitment towards ourselves and our emotional healing. Our life horrors are only the ingredients and the base recipes of our intimate emotional evolution. As a reminder, we can not change people; we

can only change the way we relate to them. The way we relate to them must be through love and the message of love. If we decide to relate to people through hate, rage, anger, resentment; we are simply throwing shit on the fan and asking to be covered by our own poo. Hate, rage, anger and resentment must be experienced and embraced as an emotional state and not expressed as a way of living, thinking, acting and reacting.

As average "Joe", when hate, rage, anger and resentment hit my mind and my body. I do my best to take a step back mentally and ask myself if the situation is for me, what do I want out of this experience and how can I grow positively out of it. This self-healing mental mechanism is available to any of us and on a personal note; it took me over thirty years to apply it as an "on-demand" awareness technique to hijack my mind out of myself created misery. Using this technique is also a way to look after our physical body. When our mental energy is captivated by emotional states such as anger and hate, our physical body is on autopilot and matches the mind process. Our heart rate, arterial tension and testosterone production increases, cortisol decreases. We produce more saliva and an array of chemicals and toxins to support our reactive behaviours. We are a living equilibrium, and automatically, all chemicals and toxins created during our rage and hate episode need to be processed and eliminated by our body. Some biology studies indicate that the quantity and quality of toxins contained within our saliva during a mental state of rage can be compared to the toxins contained within the venom of a deadly snake.

Teen Spirit

Neuroscience scientists reckon that by the age of thirty-five, we are reacting to life through a series of predictable habits at ninety-five percent of the time. Very little of the content of our life is questioned. Our living patterns are so entrenched within all cells of our body that we have robotized our human behaviours. Our primitive childhood mental processing facilities and emotional cataloguing system have upgraded themself into a new piece of coding that converts us into a limited and well-defined set of mental and emotional responses that transforms us into a self-destructing psychological machine. We are losing our emotional, creative power; we are reacting to life when, in fact, we should be acting or creating life. Reprogramming our emotional patterns is somehow engaging a war against the content stored with all cells of our body and our brain. Our physical body, through its circuitry network, has taken over our mental power. Every memory stored within our body cells is linked to our environment, and anyone included in it or forming part of it. Every memory is an emotion. We are creatures of habit and will do our utmost, through the power of repetition and the downfall of labelling, to repeat facts of the past in an automated way in our "current" present. Our emotional state is a combination of how we feel and how we think. Unfortunately, this state can be easily altered instantly and repetitively subject to how we access our memories and consequently, our emotions.

REBEL WITH PURPOSE

Our present moment, which is unique and will never repeat itself, is automatically painted by the brushes of our understanding and relationship to our memories. We are treating the present as our past. We are not living in the present moment as we are addicted to our outdated emotional content and our self-conditioning. Our future, if we do not hijack our mental patterns, will also be a representation of the past. Our role, as intelligent humans, is to reprocess our emotional content on the go and create a present and a future that is not linked to our memories and emotions. Our negative habits are giving away our free will, and more precisely, we are suffocating ourselves and our freedom. We are commenting to our slow and painful emotional suicide.

The frequency or the usage rate of our emotional patterns, habits, beliefs do not justify their truthness and authenticity. Every time that we access a memory and its linked negative, unsupportive emotions to embrace and qualify the present moment, we are only lying to ourselves and imposing a victim status on our shoulders. We are creating pain on pain. We are building a tasteless life.

Observing our human personal development cycle and life evolution, we can highlight that our teenage years are probably the most prolific in terms of challenges, growth and rewards. The transition period that converts a kid into young adults is a period where our entire life values are under scrutiny. In our quest to gain and express, unconsciously or not, our mental and emotional freedom, we are most likely to challenge whatever the world has to offer. As part of the process, we are challenging our understanding of ourselves and the way we relate to our environment and the environment itself. Our inner behavioural program and programming system have been switched to the "I deserve better" operating mode. We want changes, we want changes fast, and we will not settle for a status quo in our endeavours which are affirming our presence, identity and our unique way of thinking, living, acting and reacting.

Sadly for the majority of us, when our teenage years are over, we are settling down and, unconsciously or not, we are embracing back the norm of our living environment. The fight for freedom is over, and by the age of thirty-five, we are the product of our emotional robotization. We are reacting to life through a set of habits and premeditated reactions. We have lost our emotional creativity. We have become plain, ordinary and emotionally self-muted.

Our mind reprogramming during teenage years can be compared to the process of baking cheesecake. The cheesecake enters the oven made of a mixed combination of raw ingredients. Hopefully it will come out of the oven gold and crispy on the outside, and soft, silky and creamy on the inside. Subject to the recipe and our willingness to follow the baking direction, the skill of the baker, the oven temperature, the cooking time, our resistance to not open the oven door during the baking time, and most importantly, our care and patience during the cooling down period and unmolding process; the result should be satisfactory to some extent. Anyway, whatever the outcome, there is no chance for our creation to return on its raw form and substance. Whatever if our cake is burned, too sweet, undercooked, it will never be flour, butter, sugar ever again. Changes have occurred, and these changes are irreversible.

The period following our teenage years to our mid-thirties is somehow less flattering for the majority of us. As we settle down, this period can be compared to deflating cheesecake on a kitchen benchtop. Our teenage grandiose, oomph and vigour are getting diluted into the normality, the numbness and the comfort of life. One of the biggest downfalls of the human species is that we do not question our happiness and wellbeing status on an ongoing basis. Our teen spirit only resurfaces when it is time to fix life and its emotional crisis and dramas. Our teen spirit should be back to life daily. We should use it to create and experience the life we are only dreaming off. Our teen spirit should be brought back into our lives to subdue our behavioural and emotional laziness.

Get use to life

Life is never served to us in the same way as life is an ongoing living surprise. Whatever our astonishment or disappointment towards life and its emotional events; life always has the upper hand on us when it delivers its trueness, richness and uniqueness. We cannot control life; life is unpredictable, and this is why life is beautiful. Acknowledging with humbleness, that we have little or no control at all on life, is the best way to surrender to its beauty. Our egos lure us into false belief and distorted mental states that make us feel powerful well above life and the experience of life itself. Our robotized acknowledgement of life is dull and very basic. Our perception or interpretation of life is either a challenge or a walk in the park. Many humans have lost, or are losing, their ability to create themselves within their life and its unpredictable content. The true content of a healthy life is solely connected to our mental and emotional states. A healthy mental state of abundance has nothing to do with our buying power or stuff available on supermarket shelves. Resilience and gratitude are the key ingredients to our emotional wellbeing. Another healthy mental practice that helps us to gain a mental state of abundance is to discard the harmful habit of assumption as a living and thinking operating mode. As humans, our aim in life is to create abundance for ourselves within our life circumstances. The reactive nature of assumption limits our creative power and predefines the outcome of our life experiences and wellbeing. The way we address our emotional healing and life, in general, will have an impact on its outcome; we must be active, not reactive towards ourselves. The limitations of assumption must be converted into unlimited acts of creation. Life is served to us without a user manual; life is free. Life is total freedom; so why are we living or experiencing our life based on habits from past individual, communal or generational events. Life invites us to be disruptive and unconventional. We are invited to break away from what we called or perceived as the norm.

Life is motion; life is a perpetual and ongoing personalized motion. Nothing is or will be fixed or guaranteed forever; we need to get used to this reality. Through the evaluation of our evolution, life invites all of us to be honest and truthful towards ourselves. As a fact, we must evolve. We must declutter our mind, our life, our environments. Failing to do so; life will be delighted to send us individualized reminders on how important it is to be ourselves, and being pain-free physically, mentally, emotionally, spiritually and neurologically.

Decluttering our way of thinking, living, acting and reacting is doing an ongoing spring cleaning of our inner being memory card. Doing the "do" for the "be" will be challenging until the "be" has gained a state of abundance and will take over the "do". As a result, the "be" will perform less "do" because the bullshit that was suffocating our inner selves have disappeared as part of our neurological, physical and emotional transformations.

A few lines above, the plural was used for the word environment. During our lifetime, many types of settings will impact and shape our multi-purpose human behaviour and our insertion and level of comfort within these environments. Some of these environments can also be classified or labelled (I hate this word) as open or hidden environments. Open environments surround us and are accessible and interactive to anyone included in it, ourselves included. Open environments can be either public or private settings where all types of human interactions can happen. On the other side of the spectrum, hidden environments only exist within the frame of our unique mental existence. They are the product of our sole imagination where nobody except ourselves has access to them. Both open and hidden environments are a series of processed snapshots of our perception and interpretation of our surroundings. It is most likely that assumptions contaminate our secret environments with outdated life data, obsolete life experiences that only support our well defined emotional abilities and mental comfort, healthy or not. They are the most likely breeding grounds for the development and survival of our self-victim and self-perpetrator status. Prime examples of hidden environments are the one created by our "little" inner voice or voices, songs, movies, ethnic and family stereotypes, fears that profiled our inner conditioning into unrealistic emotional and life perspectives. Hidden environments can be compared to zoos. It looks fantastic, charming, and provides a sense of adventure. Sadly, when lockdown at night, none of the animals on display are going home at night. They have lost their autonomy, freedom and purpose. The same outcome happens when we are trapping ourselves in hidden environments. Our emotional intelligence is diminished due to our lack of cognitive fitness. We are segregating ourselves from our "own" emotional freedom.

Emotions are life fuel

Really or is it life that fuels our emotions? What is first? The chicken or the egg? Human life experiences can not exist without emotions and vice versa. Most of our interactions with the world have emotional contents, and in recent times, everything is designed and packaged to grab, arouse or abuse our emotional persona.

The world is, more than ever, a big marketing machine and this magnificent piece of human engineering is not, most of the time, a purveyor of truth. The reality of the world and the truthness of our actions, life, leisure, thoughts, dramas, traumas are polished endlessly with thick coats of fakeness, to make the reality more acceptable to our emotional sensors and our emotional anchors.

The world marketing machine does not care about our emotional wellbeing, our emotional trauma and our emotional recovery. In an environment where fakeness is promoted and rewarded, what can we expect as an outcome for our emotional sanity? The world has become a massive billboard punishing our mental wellbeing around the clock and does not offer us much rest time to recover from its pressure. Media outlets are similar to drug dealers; they got us hooked and addicted to their endless grabby emotional content that lacks human healing values.

Closer to us, there are also billboards on legs, yes the humans. Our personality types and traits define us. The majority of interactions between humans are verbal and gestural. All of us have a different approach when it comes to promote, advertise, market, or impose ourselves to a new or an existing environment and anyone included in it. When we observe our environment in terms of daily communication content, we notice that the way we communicate or interact with each other is lacking depth and substance, except if we have a common interest or goal. Most of the time, we are talking garbage to get by or to promote our importance and superiority.

The "feel-good" factor is the science used to addict us to our television set, smartphone's screens, fake news, debilitating marketing campaigns and strangely that is what is keeping us listening to crappy human stories. On the other hand, sadly, when we observe our environment, we also discover very quickly that a growing number of people are isolating themselves mentally, voluntarily or not, from human interactions.

Whatever the source of our mental hijacking, the majority of data received and processed should be discarded as soon as it enters our life and mental processing facilities. The garbage of the world becomes ours only when we decide to anchor ourselves into it. The outside noise of the world will not make us a better person. How do we feel deep down our inner-selves after hours of "feel good" benching? Have our anxiety, depression, emotional trauma vanished? Nope; there are most likely to be amplified as we are constantly distracted from our healing journey. A problem can not be solved with a problem. Emotional healing and chaotic environments, and anyone included in it are two worlds apart. Do not expect the world to keep quieter; we can not change people and their chaos. We can only change the way we relate to them and reduce as much as possible the expiry date of our emotional nuisance.

As an average "Joe", I have experienced chaos in my life and took my distance away from it. The intensity and the frequency of the mess was so intense that I started to develop withdrawal symptoms when I was away from it. I never liked it, I never enjoyed it, but I was addicted to it. Chaos was part of my mental, physical, emotional, psychological and neurological identity. So unconsciously, as the need for chaos was getting bigger within my persona, I started to create my own. For a short time, it felt home, and before I knew it, dramas filled my life. At the time, I did not have a clue or the emotional intelligence education to cope with this urge to create drama. I was lost emotionally. The two biggest realisations out of these experiences were first; a victim and a perpetrator can be within the same skin. I was beating myself to death. This acknowledgement broke my heart; it was a harrowing and teary realisation. The second one was; if we do things, ethically or not, in life that does not support and respect ourselves or our life purpose, the universe will stop us without notice in our tracks. Hurts and emotional breakdowns are guaranteed; I can write a book about it.

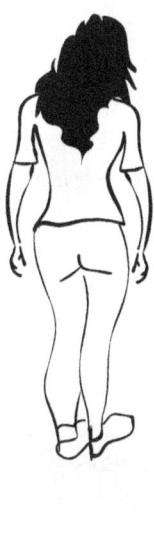

There is more to be amazed and addicted to within ourselves. So why are we afraid to face and embrace our universal inner beauty. There is no garbage, no fakeness, no fear, no trauma in our true-self. There is only us! Our emotions, the motion of life and the busyness of our environment are not present in a gained state of consciousness. We must remind ourselves that we are the mirror of the universe and more importantly, the container of its biggest best kept secrets. "I am I for I" is the portal towards our neurological healing and emotional recovery. This gateway is only accessible when we consciously disconnect ourselves from our interactions with life, productive or not, and shift our focus and energy towards our inner peace.

To belong

Our fadeaway level of consciousness that drifts us apart from our greatness is not the only factor contributing to our emotional healing hiccups and downfalls. Our expectations, just like our assumptions, will restrain us from evolving and liberating ourselves from any emotional, physical, mental and neurological setback.

When we are expecting things to be delivered in a certain way, we are turning off the creativity tap and limiting ourselves mentally to pre-framed or pre-agreed outcomes. Expectations are a form of control on ourselves and others, and it is a waste of time and energy as we have little or no control on life and others. So why bother to limit ourselves into fake mental comfort status when we can simply appreciate the magic of life and its unexpected treasures.

When we observe animals evolving in their natural environment, we realise that their survival skills and behaviours do not include expectations and assumptions. If they want something, they go and get it - no terms and conditions. They are putting themselves on the line and proceeding with their choices. Humans, on the other hand, have evolved from a survival type lifestyle to an ongoing need for comfort and instant gratification in all areas of their life. Our evolution model went from a collective to individual, and consequently, a lot of us now are living in isolation within our communities and have no or little sense of belonging.

The most significant difference between humans and animals is that we have the power of choice, the power to evolve and the power of being. All our life and without limitation, we can consciously choose, grow, change, develop, evolve and be.

As life is never served to us twice the same way, "Choose, evolve and be" is and must be a never-ending spiritual, physical, physiological, psychological, neurological and mental practice. As hard or heavy this sounds, "choose, evolve and be" can be achieved effortlessly subject to the fluidity of our mental power. When choosing a new path in life, we must acknowledge our current situation, our likes and dislike towards our current status and most importantly "what" and "why" we want to change. The "why" are the drivers in our current and future evolutions, and the "what" is the mental gap between who we currently are and our fulfilled state of being. What about the practical "how" of our inner transformation? The "how", in singular and plural form, are establishing themselves out of nowhere. Let's not overthink them; let's embrace and trust our creative healing power. The intensity of our "why", and our commitments towards them, are the catalysts to their self-developed solution and implementation. The "how" does not stand a chance to evolve without a strong "why".

As a side note: At any point and time in our life, we must be grateful towards ourselves, in a repetitive and ongoing manner, especially when the content of our life is filled with hardship and heartbreak. When we are grateful and thankful towards ourselves, poverty does not exist, and loneliness does not exist, anger does not exist, grief does not exist and so forth. Being grateful towards ourselves is pure abundance in the present moment. Practising gratefulness will trigger and stimulate our awareness. When we are living, thinking and acting in a state of consciousness, our perception of life will continuously evolve from a fixed and defined set of reacting living habits to the appreciation of an unlimited amount of new perspectives and opportunities for our being.

The practice of gratefulness is also an easy and efficient way to heal and release the layers of our emotional footprint ingrained within our entire physical body and not only the parts that catch our selective attention and nurturing.

Gratefulness is a genuine form of emotional surrender.

Under a basic form of observation, "to belong" and "belonging" can be acknowledged as a state of mind and a little piece of individual coding inside our neurological system, that defines us as being a part of something such as family, community, team or a circle of friends. Subject to the quality of our emotional and mental content, this piece of coding will be filled, or not, with expectations and assumptions that will rule our approach, experience and integration within any types of environments and their potential evolutions.

One of the best examples nature has on offer in terms of evolution in motion is the chameleon. As a member of the lizard's family, chameleons have a highly developed ability to change colour and appearance on the go. As a result, they can blend and to be part of any ever-changing environments; no questions asked. Their survival transformation is automated. They are permitting themselves to let go of something in preparation to embrace new life experiences even without knowing if this new experience will be beneficial to them.

Humans also have the mental power to blend into new and existing environments, and most importantly, they have the power to create new environments too. "To belong" and "belonging" will not be served to us on a silver plate. It is our responsibility to evolve to get what is beneficial to us; even if this means withdrawing ourselves from unfilling environments and anyone included in it. Withdrawing does not mean going into an isolation mode or cutting contacts with our communities and society. Withdrawing means being active mentally to preserve our emotional sanity to avoid, at any cost, falling back into primitive and reactive survival living patterns. One door closes, and another one opens with the universal grace, synchronicity and blessing of life.

Dessert

Dessert — Acknowledgments

At the end of a meal, dessert always creates excitement; children of all ages will be delighted, if allowed, to start their meal with their preferred indulgence. Now, we all can! We are giving ourselves the permission and the freedom to put back the sweetest or saltiness into our daily emotional landscape. Best dessert for me is a bowl of warm vegetable and chicken broth served with fresh black cracked pepper. So good!

In our dessert section, only one item on the menu. An empty five compartments Bento box.

Empty! Five compartments to be consumed as much as we want and as often as possible. Yeah, I can feel the excitement in the room! Yeah, you must play the emotional healing game to win it!

The Bento box is a single-player emotional healing awareness game. The aim of the game is to fill the five compartments of the Bento Box. On average, only two to five minutes are required to play a session, and a one-hour interval is needed between gaming sessions. Fully committed, twelves sessions a day is ideal. There is no age requirement to play the Bento Box!

Two to five minutes of our time is required every hour, from 7.00 am to 7.00 pm. An awareness alarm on our watch, mobile phone, computer and tablet is handy. As a single-player game, we are accountable to ourselves! This game is about "I" and "I" only.

How does the Bento box emotional healing awareness game work?

The game starts with an empty box every time we play. We aim of the game is to fill the five compartments of the bento box in the following order are:

Compartment One: Breakaway!

Compartment Two: Be grateful!

Compartment Three: Celebrate our choices!

Compartment Four: Create new!

Compartment Five: Vibrate our outcome!

Life is an art, and as the creative director of our emotional content, we need to give ourselves the time and space for valuable change. Play the game without deep and meaningful questioning; our emotional evolution is well above meaningless answers to outdated questions. Let's the spontaneity of our young inner child to be the player.

Compartment One: Breakaway!

Our daily emotional life is a mirror of our internal and intimate self-created operating system. This cycle needs to be hacked. Our emotional and mental behaviours must be brought to the daylight regularly, and our automated brain popping patterns must be interrupted.

For a few seconds, we take time to acknowledge our thoughts, feelings and emotional contents on the go. Just checking, what is going on in the present moment and the present moment only!

No question, no judgement, just developing our awareness skills and creating little interruptions in our well embedded emotional habits.

Action:

Fill the first compartment of the Bento box with at least five "I am breaking away…" items.

Compartment Two: Be grateful!

The state of gratefulness is a powerful mental, emotional, physical and neurological circuit breaker. Our entire being is on hold when we are grateful and appreciative towards ourselves. Grateful is humility in the now.

Action:

Fill the second compartment of the Bento box with at least five "I am grateful for..." items.

Compartment Three: Celebrate our choices!

Celebrating our life and emotional choices is also a form of gratitude. When celebrating our choices, we are celebrating everything that usually supports us to grow in our daily life and emotional journey. Celebrating our choices helps us to develop our emotional awareness and self-develop new code lines in our emotional triggers.

Action:

Fill the third compartment of the Bento box with at least five "I am celebrating..." items.

Compartment Four: Create new!

The two most significant powers available to any single human being living on earth today are the power of choice and the power of creation. We have infinite and endless options available around the clock to create and develop a truthful, genuine and authentic self.

All of us, without exclusion, have the power to create a new self on the go. Life choices have an expiry date, and now we are free to create our ideal emotional being.

Action:

Fill the fourth compartment of the Bento box with at least five "My new self is ...; my new choices are..." items.

Note: Our soul is the one filling the Bento Box, not our ego.

Compartment Five: Vibrate our outcome!

"Vibrate our outcome" is the necessary step for our complete and interconnected physical, emotional, spiritual and neurological self to experience the desired outcome to its fullest prior it realises or materialises in the real world.

"Vibrate it until it is true."

Vibrating our new selves is embedding their positive and uplifting changes through our entire body. Every cell, neurone, skin tissue and atom must resonate to the projection of the new "us" well before we become.

When we vibrate, our body frequency changes automatically reprocess our neurological and emotional content. We are new, and we can be new every second of any given day!

"Vibrate it until it is true" versus "Fake it until it is true". "Vibrate" has a healing content that is happening. When we vibrate, we are in charge and committed to our emotional healing. We are emotionally in motion; our outdated operating system is getting the correct "self-love" update.

By contrast, when we fake it, our endeavour is contentless. We are like porn actors, with our legs spread in the air, screaming our lungs out and feeling nothing. In a faking state, we are physically, mentally, physiology, neurologically, spiritually and emotionally absent. When we fake our emotional destiny; We are exhausting ourselves of precious emotional energy.

How to vibrate our new emotional self to experience, intimately, the desired outcomes of our new emotional and life choices?

The first step is to include ourselves! All about the "I".

We are the creative directors of our emotional contents; we are the ones who select our life psychological ingredients. We must choose ingredients that support ourselves in our emotional evolution and invite us to vibrate our projected selves. Studies now prove that the majority of people that are watching craft videos on social media are gaining excellent skills without any formal and technical training. These people are vibrating as they are projecting themselves into the content of the video. Repeating our experience through all our body senses (touch, sight, hearing, smell and taste) will validate the new experience as our new, and authentic, reality within our entire neurological system.

Action:

The fifth compartment of the Bento box is about creating our "inclusive" well-crafted movie that invites all our senses to our emotional evolution. The content of the video must be filled with details that reflect our personal and individual new emotional and life choices. Our aim is to create the ideal "I" life movie. When done, let's enjoy watching our new selves. Let's feel, touch, smell, taste and hear the new "I" evolving freely within their environment and anyone included in it. As we become familiar with our new senseful "I"; we are vibrating, attracting and embracing our unlimited physical, emotional, spiritual and neurological potential as our new reality.

The Success of this technique is the evolution of the "create, watch and vibrate" process. It is not a one-off session and practise will make us better at it. Each time we fill the fifth compartment of our Bento Box, let's go a little bit deeper, let's add relevant details, let's add softness to ourselves, let's cut our sharp edges, let's be "I" with a smile on our face.

After Dinner

Less is more. As "average" Joe, I had first encountered this sentence while I was studying architecture at University. As a new mind experience, the sentence and its content bug and disturb me for a while. How can less be more? Average "Joe" as a young registered and practising architect, many moons ago, "less is more" became the creative force behind my architectural concept and design. My work philosophy was not to achieve architectural purity; I aimed to value all constraints imposed on an architectural problem and

to suggest a stripped-down architectural solutions that enhance the architectural space and the spatial experiences of its end users.

An architectural space is simply a series of walls, ceilings and floors containing a few openings from which an ever-changing light is coming through casting ever-changing shadows. The art of placing, correctly, walls and openings will define the tension within architectural spaces, its perception and emotional impact on an end-user.

Not much is required to create quality architectural spaces; the same rule applies to our emotional space. We are creating our walls, our floors, our ceiling, our lights and our shadows. As we build, we experience! There is no need to build castles and fortresses to protect ourselves emotionally. A healthy emotional space requires the right balance between openings and walls. Our emotional architectural fluidity can simply be achieved by embracing a constructive and deconstructive approach. Less is more!

The Bill

What To Do When Our Emotions Hurt

What is the real cost, individually and collectively, for not taking care of our emotional and mental health?

Being long enough on mother Earth, I can confirm that there is no free lunch in life. Everything has a price except for items that are impossible to purchase off the shelves from a general store or supermarket. Self-directed kindness does not cost a penny! "I love myself", "I believe in myself" will not cost us a dime. It is free and available "on-demand" around the clock!

On the other hand, not taking care of ourselves emotionally and mentally can lead to life's unwanted and undesired side effects. Our emotional footprint is imprinted into our physical, emotional, mental, spiritual and neurological selves, and its healthiness is linked to our daily quality of life. Ignoring ourselves, emotionally, could cost us big on short, medium and long term. To clarify, the word "cost" is not only related to financial matters; emotional ignorance and arrogance are damaging, and sometimes destroying friendships, families, businesses, relationships, aspirations and dreams. Letting individual and collective honesty prevails, emotional healing must be our number one priority in our daily existence.

When we are taking the time to observe our environment and any included in it, we become aware of the mechanics of our emotional surroundings. Human habits are predictable. Without much training, we all can read the sorrow, the misery, the anxiety, the depression, the fear on someone else's face and body posture. Equally, they can do the same; they can visualise our emotional health on display. Our physical body is the mirror and the projection of our emotional being. When we project positive emotional energy, we invite and attract positive emotional energy into our inner world. Emotional opportunities are created. We are growing and vibrating without much effort.

Unfortunately, emotional energy is a form of segregation. We can reject or isolate others because of their emotional contents, and by the same token, they can reject or isolate us because of our emotional vibrational frequencies. Associating ourselves with like-minded peoples is a crucial factor to our healthy emotional evolution. Embracing and challenging our emotional content will make us humble, healthy and attractive vibrational "leaders".

Let the power of our mind be with us!

I love myself. I believe in myself.

I love myself. I believe in myself.

I love myself. I believe in myself.

I love myself. I believe in myself.

I love myself. I believe in myself.

I love myself. I believe in myself.

The Mint

In some restaurants, complimentary mint flavoured lollies land on our table with the well-folded bill at the end of our meal. They are breath enhancers, refreshers and a subtle reminder that our dining experience is coming to an end and an invitation to proceed with our day!

Similar to a dining experience, emotional healing is a one-way adventure; when started, there is no way back! On the other hand and contrary to a dining experience, emotional healing has no ending. When we are facing our emotional or psychological bills; there are no lollies. The refresher and the sweetness of life are self-created and starts within the healthiness of our emotional content. Let's embrace ourselves; let's love ourselves and let's believe in ourselves as no one can ever do it better than we possibly do! As a fact, there are no guarantees in a self-healing journey and by the same token; there are no guarantees in life either whatever society tries to impose on us. When we are aware that the only guarantee on offer is that there is no guarantee at all; we have nothing to lose and everything to gain.

We are free!

Attracting and preserving our emotional freedom and peace is not a passive matter. We must be active to protect and preserve our emotional and mental being; we have no choice! In life, whatever the size of our entourage and their support, we are a single-player in our emotional battlefields. Within ourselves, the universe's secrets are there to be experienced; loving ourselves is one of them!

Let's become an active player in the "Bento Box" healing army and become a confident vibrational leader.

Doggy Bag

An alternative useful and practical way to learn to vibrate emotionally is by humming. When we are humming, we are making a low and steady continuous sound that symbolises the vibrational frequency of our neurological and emotional state in the present moment.

As a practice run, let's hum a negative life experience for a minute and soon after, let's hum its joyful opposite. How does it feel? Now let's push this practice to the next level. Let's start humming the vibrational frequency of an unsupportive state mind and transition without stopping humming to our preferred and desired emotional outcome. It feels good quickly without much effort!

With practice, it is near impossible to hum negativity! If invited, our brain will jump automatically to our positive vibrational frequency and ignore the low hands of our emotional contents.

Namaste.

www.ingramcontent.com/pod-product-compliance
Lightning Source LLC
Chambersburg PA
CBHW022018290426
44109CB00015B/1216